Finding Sanctuary in Nature

Finding Sanctuary in Nature

*Simple Ceremonies
in the Native American Tradition
for Healing Yourself and Others*

Jim PathFinder Ewing
(Nvnehi Awatisgi)

FINDHORN PRESS

First published by Findhorn Press 2007

ISBN 978-1-84409-095-2

British Library Cataloguing-in-Publication Data.
A catalogue record for this book is available from the British Library.

Edited by Ellen Kleiner, Blessingway
Proof-read by Magaer Lennox
Cover design by Damian Keenan
Illustrations by Annette Waya Ewing
Layout by Pam Bochel
Printed in the USA

2 3 4 5 6 7 8 9 10 11 12 13 12 11 10

A portion of royalties from the sale of each book will be donated to
Native American and other organizations dedicated to spiritual teachings.

Published by
Findhorn Press
117–121 High Street
Forres IV36 1AB
Scotland, UK

t +44-(0)1309 690582
f +44-(0)131 777 2711
e info@findhornpress.com

www.findhornpress.com

To the Powers
who aid us in fulfilling our potential
as Children of Earth and Sky

We are Children of Earth and Sky—
Our bodies, of Mother Earth
Our souls, of divine light.
We walk between the worlds,
As cocreators of the universe
In this instant of eternity.

Contents

Preface

This book was written not to indoctrinate readers into a particular way of viewing the world but to offer a broader way of seeing that can be the basis for healing and wholeness of individuals and the Earth. There is no one way, since as individuals we must each find our own way. We are all Children of Earth and Sky, beings with incredible powers, but in our society the innate abilities of people are often not acknowledged or appreciated. While I was growing up in the 1950s, shamanism or the medicine way was not recognized in mainstream America, and there weren't many avenues for children with the ability to see in dreams, foretell the future, or divine the way of things.

Fortunately, this situation is changing and methods are now taught for developing innate abilities and unique visions. Most are categorized as "New Age," though many are thousands of years old. With the advent of new media—twenty-four-hour satellite and cable television, the Internet, e-mail, and Web sites—the world appears to be shrinking and the transmission of information has become instantaneous. The Internet may indeed be the precursor for a time when we all will be connected in a grid of common communication and understanding using the expanded abilities of what we now call shamanism or the medicine way, as suggested by ancient prophecies. Until then, it behooves each of us to develop as best we can, learning as much as possible, and becoming men and women of knowledge.

Over the years, it has been an honor and a privilege to have had teachers from various Native American tribes, including Cherokee, Choctaw, Yokuts, Lakota, Mayan, Iroquois, and Diné, along with some followers of Eastern spiritual paths. One of my teachers, Reiki master William Lee Rand, who founded the International Center for Reiki Training, said that he approached Reiki as a skeptic, desiring to see if it worked before adopting it. Indeed, the real test of any training or practice is its ability to empower you, provide a means for understanding life's many energetic forces, lead to a supportive view of life and the world, and foster the development of innate abilities to the highest capacity. The purpose of this book is to help readers achieve each of these goals well enough to clarify their unique vision.

A major concern in writing this book was how best to present Native American traditions and their role in today's world. I ultimately decided to avoid giving specific information about tribal ceremonies for three reasons: specific ceremonies belong to their respective, specific tribes; the ceremonies would have little meaning or power for people unfamiliar with the tribal traditions; and the book's purpose is to help you find your *own* ceremonies, practices that have special meaning for you and give you your own power.

Many people today with no personally meaningful ceremonies in their lives adopt the ceremonies of others, hoping for empowerment. But that is a false hope and it would be fruitless to aid in that path. For example, there is a beautiful and effective Cherokee curing ceremony that involves calling the Deer Spirits to aid in a patient's recovery that could have been set down in this book. But without the understanding of the words or the cultural milieu in which the ceremony originated, one speaking the indecipherable words and performing the unfathomable actions would not allow for connecting with the necessary healing Powers; the gap between the worlds would be too great. That's because it is *people* who give power to *words* and *actions*. Just as prayers from the heart have power because they carry intent, ceremonies require they are performed in concert with the Creator and therefore consummated with full awareness.

At the same time, the anger expressed by many Native Americans about their ceremonies being "stolen" by outsiders or tainted by their use of them often derives from a lack of understanding regarding the positive role these ancient traditions can play in today's world. Such individuals view their heritage as a possession that can be stolen when in fact heritage cannot be stolen—although it can become lost. Ceremonies that have become meaningful only as historical or cultural artifacts will definitely be lost; the ways practiced and lived, on the other hand, will change, like all living things. Outsiders who adopt native ways and use them for a little while before passing them on may in fact be contributing in a positive way to this change. The ancient ceremonies are not museum pieces, dead and lifeless, unless we make them so by robbing them of their vitality by keeping them as objects, rather than honoring them as living, changing, and growing through use and expression. People who understand the ancient ways should delight in seeing them flourish everywhere and grow stronger.

Additionally, some people complain that the ceremonies being practiced today are not authentic enough. When at a recent Green Corn Festival a man complained about this, I asked him how committed he was to precisely following the ancient traditions. Was he prepared to strip naked in front of the gathering and be scratched from head to toe with a seven-toothed comb until his blood ran freely? Was he willing to set aside a week to ten days every three months for fasting, prayer, and dancing all day and night, not just on occasional weekends and the few days he could get off work? Was he ready to go into the woods and kill deer for the people, cutting out the animals' tongues for sacred ceremony? Practicing the old ceremonies in the old way reflects a commitment to perpetuating a lifestyle, whereas adapting the ceremonies to today's world reflects a promise to honor the spirit of the ancestors by carrying their teachings forward to new generations. Longevity of the old ways, as opposed to hidebound authenticity, is the greater gift and is achieved by continually giving life to them so they may flourish everywhere, among all people, and thus endure.

Suzanne Dupree, a Miniconjou Sioux pipe carrier known as Looking Back Woman, has spoken out about how "protection" of the ancient ways is being used to lend them an exclusivity that is at odds with their true nature. She notes that in the old days, women shared spiritual power with men and were given the duty of ensuring the continuation of sacred ways from generation to generation. But today, she points out, most medicine people are men who are making decisions without the input of women, including the elder women—the traditional wisdom keepers of the tribes—even though it was a woman, White Buffalo Calf Woman, who gave the sacred pipe to the Lakota people.

Further, Dupree has decried such edicts as the "Protection of Ceremonies," in which a number of Lakota men, not a single woman among them, proclaimed that only people who were Lakota or Sioux Oyate (people) and carried certificates of blood quantum issued by the federal government could perform or authorize ceremonies, and that they must be conducted in Lakota, stating:

> *How can anyone say who is or is not qualified to perform ceremonies? Is it not the Creator who touches one's heart and calls them to the altar? By demanding language, blood quantum, and other self-serving requirements, dogma and doctrine are being injected into our spiritual ways where none existed for thousands of years. We must not tell people what they must believe.*
>
> *By closing the door to our faith and ancient rites to "outsiders," the Proclamation closes the Sacred Hoop that is supposed to include all life. Instead of having compassion for the thousands of people worldwide who sincerely wish to learn the ceremonies, they are met with a closed fist. Instead of taking the awesome task to teach them, the writer of the Proclamation wants to corner the market and dictate who may or may not come into the circle.*[1]

It is imperative for the survival of our world that medicine teachings be shared, as the late Frank Fools Crow, an Oglala medicine man, said: "Survival of the world depends on our sharing what we have, and working together. If we do not, the whole world will die. First the planet, and next the people."[2]

Nor was or is he alone in this view. As White Bison, the native wellbriety group, has stressed over the years, native people were given knowledge of the natural world in order to share it, and were told by the Creator in ancient times: "You will be keepers of Mother Earth. Among you I will give the wisdom about nature, about the interconnectedness of all things, about balance, and about living in harmony. You Red People will see the secrets of nature. You will live in hardship and the blessing of this is you will stay close to the Creator. The day will come when you will need to share the secrets with the other people of the Earth because they will stray from their spiritual ways."[3]

The late Mad Bear Anderson, an Iroquois medicine man, emphasized how Native American spirituality could function to mediate between religions of the East and West, thereby increasing harmony on Earth: "The Eastern religions represent spirituality that looks inward. The Western religions represent spirituality that tends to look outward. We are the people whose spirituality is of the middle. We stand for the sacrality of Nature, for the sacred ways of the Earth. Therefore, we can be mediators between East and West, reminding the others that Nature is holy and full of the Great Spirit."[4]

Peter V. Catches, a 38th generation Lakota medicine man who today carries forward the ancient teachings of the Spotted Eagle Way, has explained: "Living in a world full of prejudice, we have to look inward to find the true nature of ourselves. Now is the time to change and move toward enlightenment, to extinguish our old fears of one another. When the beacon of loving light burns bright in our once dark and lonely domain, we will beat the drums of unity and shout its songs."[5]

None other than the late Martha Bad Warrior, keeper of the White Buffalo Calf Pipe Bundle of the Sioux Oyate, said, "This heritage is such as to be open in the good of all mankind, regardless of race, creed, color..."[6]

These leading voices of Native American people of the past and present should be heeded, and history tells us why. For the past five hundred years, Western culture has dominated the Earth with its values of patriarchy, materialism, exclusion, domination, and hierarchy, resulting in serious imbalances. Consequently, the native ways, which stress balance through inclusion, coexistence, and unity, are sorely needed in the world today.

We each must come forward to share what we know. My name, *Nvnehi Awatisgi* (Cherokee, new-nay-hee a-WAT-is-gee) was given to me by a Keetowah (Cherokee) spiritual elder. It is both a name and an obligation. It means, one who finds the path; and it is usually given to someone who has been down many paths, good ones and not-so-good ones, so that counsel may be trusted based on wisdom and experience. In native way, one of the greatest honors a person may receive is to be given a name that was carried well by someone in the past. This name was held by a Cherokee chief who died in 1827, and led his people well. But the name also has a higher purpose, or spiritual impetus. Path, *nvnehi,* also means "the immortals." It is the obligation of the person who holds this name not only to help others find the best path for them, but the highest path, the path to the immortals. That is my hope and prayer with this book.

Although the title of the book says these teachings are in the Native American tradition, there are many traditions, as many as there were tribes, bands, and peoples before European conquest. The ceremonies presented, and others like them, emphasize the positive qualities of inclusion, unity, and spirituality—and thus can help us bring balance to ourselves and our Earth. These principles are in fact at the heart of all major religious traditions, though they may be overshadowed by various political prejudices and practices. They are in nature and in our nature, waiting only to be tapped to provide sanctuary, healing, and wholeness.

Wisatologi nihi! ("Many blessings on your path!")

Getting Started

The world we inhabit is filled with spaces that hold turmoil or peace, sorrow or happiness. Some places can make us feel chaotic and troubled, while others have us feeling serene and uplifted. But we are not mere puppets of the forces around us, subject to energies beyond our control. We can choose our realities, finding the source of creation within and allowing it to radiate out into the physical world, reordering our environments. Similarly, we can actively create spaces in nature that promote serenity, healing, and wholeness in order to have sanctuary.

Although the stereotype of nature is a wilderness scene, wherever we might be, whether in a rural area or the most populated city, nature is all around, as well as within, us. And around us nature can be found not only in landscapes such as mountains, beaches, oceans, deserts, prairies, lakes, streams, hills, and jungles, but also in backyards, vacant city lots, and even garden rooms or potted plants in homes or office interiors.

The key to finding sanctuary in nature for a healing space and tranquility is in how we connect with nature, both internally and externally. To create a meaningful connection, it is necessary to recognize that you yourself contain forces of nature and to understand how the forces of nature within you interact with the forces of nature without. Ultimately, finding sacred spaces in nature to do simple ceremonies for healing yourself and others does not require esoteric skills or the intervention of an expert. Anyone can connect with the powerful forces of nature internally and externally through the assistance of guides and spirit helpers, which requires only comprehension of the spiritual principles involved, a few tools that are easily obtained or fashioned, and knowledge of some basic techniques. All that is needed to be successful are an open mind and heart and a willingness to face the unknown so you can "come home" to nature.

This book provides information about the principles, tools, and techniques necessary to help you harness the power of nature for making healing ceremonies. Included are instruction and exercises to develop capabilities for connecting with power animals as guides, building a medicine wheel, and retrieving and integrating lost soul pieces, and more. Readers are encouraged to keep a notebook of observations that might prove useful in discovering new avenues for inner discovery; entries from my own notebook are provided as samples.

The first three chapters of this book conclude with a short review of major points for easy reference, including key search words to find more material about related topics on the Internet. The fourth chapter provides a compendium of ceremonies with details about how to perform them using the principles, tools, and techniques revealed in the first three chapters. The book concludes with a glossary of terms specific to doing ceremony. In addition, the Web site Healing the Earth/ Ourselves, at http://www.blueskywaters.com, offers books, CDs, tools, and additional reading material that may be ordered by mail or e-mail, as well as periodic classes and workshops.

If you absorb the information presented in these pages and practice the ceremonies described, your inner life and perspective on the world around you will change. You will likely experience healing and peace on many levels and also the love and joy that comes from giving these gifts to others and the Earth.

Chapter One

Finding Sacred Space Within

Only within burns the fire I kindle.
My heart the altar.
My heart the altar.
— Unidentified Buddhist Nun

The first step in finding sanctuary in nature to prepare for ceremony is to find the sacred space within. Although this step is fundamental to doing any type of ceremony, people frequently do not focus intently enough on it to become adept at it. In fact, finding sacred space within can sometimes be more difficult for experienced practitioners than for novices, because novices often believe they cannot do it properly and thus exert a great deal of energy on the task, while "experts" tend to think that since past experiences revealed sacred space already existing within them they need no longer strive to access it. The goal lies between the two extremes—to exercise focused intent without preconceived notions.

To do this, care must be taken to prevent ego or personality from getting in the way, since ceremony requires an almost "egoless state," as Eastern traditions describe it. While it is necessary to acknowledge the significance of the ego as a survival mechanism, it is also important to understand how the ego can cause us to see everything in terms of the self, leading to selfishness and a distorted view of the world. Personality, which includes ego, demonstrates who we think we are rather than who we actually are—a critical distinction. Westerners often have difficulty embracing the concept of an egoless state, upon which most meditative and spiritual practices are established. To better understand this notion, imagine a bird effortlessly floating on the wind, directing the currents of flight with a single flick of its wing tip, then see the bird as who you are in your most egoless state, with its wings as intent and the wind as the power of nature all around you.

Consensus Reality versus Nonordinary Reality

In addition to attaining an egoless state, to find a sacred space within for creating ceremony we must allow for the existence, beyond everyday consensus reality, of a more all-encompassing nonordinary reality that is the basis for the occurrence of miracles and all wisdom traditions. Toltec shamanism, for example, maintains that presences and events just as real as the ones we perceive can enter our perceived reality when we allow for their existence. Our consensus reality, or all that is known or named, is called the *tonal* (TONE-all), whereas the nonordinary reality, or all that can be, is known as the *nagual* (NAHw'all).[1] The dimension of the nagual tends to be far more expansive than our normal restricted notions of reality.

Consider this image: If your consciousness is a wide-beamed light, everything within the circle of the light is the tonal, and everything both within the circle of light and beyond is the nagual. To embrace this view is to live in a world of infinite possibilities in which you are able to perceive—and influence—anything seen or unseen, known or unknown; and a person who does so is often called a nagual. To do ceremony, it is important to embrace the idea that you have the ability to become a nagual and that the guides, angels, and higher powers, which we call the Powers because they are immortal, will support you in becoming who you truly are—a being who is one with all creation.

There are techniques for determining when an individual is perceiving the nagual as opposed to the tonal. Foremost among them is learning to discern when you are operating from your authentic self (who you are) rather than your personality (who you think you are). Developing this ability is the focus of many rituals, including long, lonely vigils called vision quests or pipe fasts. Such periods of isolation on a mountain, in a pit, or some other secluded place, teach an individual to recognize when the authentic self is operative and what is "really real."

A simple technique for determining "who's in charge"—your authentic self or your personality—to observe responses to the self-talk going on in your head. Our self-talk derives from our personality, which has been formed by the influential figures in our lives, such as parents, teachers, bosses, peers, and schoolmates; so you can safely assume such influences have taken over when you hear voices in your head telling you how to think or act, or judging your intent. This chatter can be self-destructive and inhibiting, diverting you from doing what you know is good for you or what you most deeply want.

From the "Voices" to the Stillpoint

Self-talk is often so ingrained, it prevents us from exploring new ways of thinking and being—and thus growing. For example, a common type of "voice" is that of "the realist" persona grounded in the idea that nothing exists unless it is rigorously proven beyond a shadow of a doubt. This way of perceiving things forms the basis of science, logic, and pragmatism. But it excludes most of reality because very little of what actually occurs in the universe can be objectively measured, and even then, as physics itself has proven, the act of observation changes the object observed. Rather than exercising the spirit of discovery that is the aim of science, people who follow such a voice use limited knowledge to discourage new ideas and explain away the unknown.

In truth, if we incorporate only what is known and believed to be knowable into our field of awareness and our perception of reality, we are limiting our universe to only a fraction of what may exist and excluding the miracles, which are part of nature itself. Moreover, if we do not allow for events unknown and unexpected, we will not see or appreciate them when they appear.

Even scientists recognize the inherent bias of science as reflected in what is called the "random rat" syndrome, according to which if ninety-nine out of one hundred experiments result in the same outcome, the one that distorts correlations will routinely be thrown out. Indeed, if it were not for the force behind all material reality, which cannot be quantified or measured, as it is infinite and unknowable—what some Native Americans call the Great Mystery, Creator, or God—there would be no science.

The voice of "the realist" is so pervasive in Western culture that virtually everyone to a greater or lesser degree has it. It serves the useful purpose of keeping us functioning in a three-dimensional world with other physical beings who share our consensus reality. It keeps us fearful, however, purporting as it does to protect us from possible harm related to anything that has not already been tried with a successful result. In helping maintain the status quo, it ultimately prevents growth and a broader experience of life. For this reason, in shamanism the ego persona, epitomized by the realist, is often portrayed as a separate entity whose purpose is not in our best interest, and who must be tricked or circumvented if we are to gain insight into what is really real and discover the authentic self. Thus, to find the authentic self it is necessary to recognize that the voices you hear are not you but rather limited personae with their own agendas. As virtually all wisdom traditions teach, the real you is the silence within, the space known as the Stillpoint. And who you really are is the one who listens discerningly to the voices in your head.

Your response to these voices determines who is in control. If you listen to them and act on them, then your personality is in control. But if you listen to them and let them fade away, or consciously choosing your behavior, you are being your authentic self operating from your

5

sacred space. The goal in preparing for ceremony is to remain unaffected by the "what ifs," "buts," and fears of self-talk, and learn to act while connected to that space.

Tricking the Trickster

Our personality keeps us from finding the sacred space within through several devices rooted primarily in fear. These devices can be seen as tricks played on us by our personality to keep us from discovering who we really are and acting from our authentic self. Various religions and spiritual paths, aware of this dynamic, teach that the first hurdle to be crossed in living the spiritual life is paralysis by fear. Conquering fear can be such a great challenge that many people seeking to follow a spiritual path eventually give up—and for good reason. Overcoming fear is an impossible task, since fear can take as many forms or masks as one's personality can invent for it. To overcome personality, the generator of all these fears, we must become aware of how it tricks us and then outsmart it, or trick *it*.

A way to understand how personality functions is to explore the tradition of the Trickster figure in Native American cultures. The Trickster appears in a variety of guises: he is known as Raven among tribes of the American Northwest, as Coyote among Western tribes, as Rabbit among the Cherokee (Tsalagi) in the Eastern United States, and by various other names in other cultures around the world. The Trickster always knows more than humans yet is ultimately tricked by his own games. A beautiful Apache story, for example, illustrates how the Trickster Coyote goes around the world naming things until an immortal who existed before the earth was formed, Boy of the Water, steps out from behind a bush next to a stream and tells him that someone is coming who will be the namer of things, taking his place as the premier being of the earth. Coyote is concerned and asks, "Will I die?" The immortal tells him, "No, there will be many hardships and Coyote will suffer, along with all beings of the Earth, but Coyote will never die."

As this tale reminds us, the Trickster Coyote will remain with us humans, no matter how we shape our world.[2] Our personality, our wily wild nature, will never die, even though it may change shapes, forms, and masks repeatedly. Likewise our authentic self, the space within where sacredness resides and from which we can do ceremony, will also always exist. We need only become one with it, allowing life's momentary illusions—the endless distractions devised to keep us from focusing on it—to fade away through our awareness of them. We are, after all, now the namers of things, not Coyote, and it is our sacred duty to bring right order to the world.

Seeing the personality as the Trickster helps us gain perspective on its antics to be able to dismiss them, not out of fear or anger but with awareness and understanding. From this vantage point, it becomes clear that the personality keeps us functioning in the three-dimensional world in which we are comfortable; as such, it is a reality but not the only reality. It is a place from which we can act and react but not the only place. We can also act from the sacred space within.

Exercise 1 Accessing the Stillpoint

The Stillpoint is the sacred space from which all creativity derives and all ceremony is done. To access the Stillpoint is to "be still and know," a state that becomes more attainable the more relaxed one is. A simple way to access the Stillpoint is through meditation, and an easy way to meditate is to clasp your hands in front of you in the prayer position and gaze at the middle fingers.[3]

Your personality will attempt to sneak into your consciousness and divert you in any number of ways; don't be distracted or allow emotions such as anger to surface. Just gently brush the thoughts away, laughing at the Trickster, until you find stillness and peace. Practicing this exercise makes it easier to access the Stillpoint, finding the sacred space within, from which to do ceremony.

The sacred space from which you operate to do sacred ceremony is the space within which the Creator resides, the altar of your life. When you are in that place of power, you realize that what is really real is much more subtle, profound, and powerful than any dramatic external phenomenon. It is there that you are the "still, small voice" at one with the Creator—and in effect, a cocreator.

Often we expect Creator, God, or a universal spiritual force to be evident in dramatic ways. An illustration that the power of the sacred can be subtle rather than dramatic occurs in a favorite Bible verse in I Kings 19: 4–12, which tells how Elijah fled into the wilderness fearing for his life, and an angel fed him and told him to await the coming of the Lord at Mount Horeb: "And behold, the Lord passed by, and a great and strong wind rent the mountains, and broke in pieces the rocks before the Lord, but the

Lord was not in the wind; and after the wind an earthquake, but the Lord was not in the earthquake; and after the earthquake a fire, but the Lord was not in the fire; and after the fire a still small voice...." This passage emphasizes how powerful forces can be expressed in subtle ways. Imagine the power the cycle of the seasons has on instinctual animal behavior. In the Arctic north of the Americas, for instance, the caribou travel hundreds of miles from their wintering spots as small bands, gathering at the sound of the wind to head to their summer grounds, where in spring the cows all drop their calves at the same time—50,000 in a single day. Similarly powerful yet silent forces are at play when a field of flowers blooms in spring or when frost withers a crop in winter.

When we stand before the altar of our life, in awe of the subtlety and power of nature, we are in the sacred space within. From here we can do ceremony, empowered as we are to heal ourselves, others, and the Earth.

Listen for the still, small voice in all you do. It is there, beneath the thunder, not overshadowed by the lightning, nor dimmed by the brightest sunlight. It is there, always.

From the Energy Notebook:
I Befriend Rabbit

A number of years ago, it seemed everything in my life was going wrong. Wherever I looked, all was bad; everything I did went awry. It was if the Trickster Coyote was always around. He always teaches by his tricks, though they are often hard lessons. (At the time, I did not know that these mistakes were made memorable so I would not repeat them and thus endanger my survival.) About this time, I visited Tallequah, Oklahoma, the capital of the Cherokee Nation. There I met an artist who had in his shop window a truly magical, large image of Rabbit, the Trickster of the Cherokee, that he had created from plywood and paint. I was transfixed; it was as if some still, small voice were speaking to my soul. When I asked if I could buy it, he told about Rabbit's tricks, known to him from Cherokee tales, some of which I remembered hearing in my youth. Rabbit, like Coyote, is definitely a Trickster, but Rabbit's tricks are gentler, usually poking fun at himself, where we learn our lessons, rather than the harsh lessons of Coyote, who we laugh at, but with the laugh that is not joy, but deep-felt sorrow. Finally, he said, "I'm not sure you want Rabbit in your life, but if you really do I'll sell it."

Since that time I have kept Rabbit in a prominent place in my home. I frequently say hello to him, and laugh ruefully at the things he brings to my life, sometimes through personal hurt and sorrow. From this experiment, I have learned that although we cannot avoid the Trickster we can become aware that he is not an enemy but a potential ally who shows us our weaknesses and helps us grow. We cannot escape who we are, good and bad, and the more we reject what might seem like a negative aspect of ourselves—what some call the shadow self—the more insistently it will make its presence known. We give homage to the Trickster in this way, befriending it.

Josef Stalin's advice to keep our friends close and our enemies closer applies to our relationship with the Trickster. It is useful to befriend him, to allow him to help you, to laugh and be accepting of yourself rather than fearful, to grow in awareness rather than remain imprisoned by fear and limited perspective.

Review

How to find the sacred space within:

- Recognize that your thoughts, the voices in your head, are not your authentic self.
- Don't be distracted or diverted by "what ifs," "buts," judgments, or fears.
- Recognize your personality as an ally, but also as a trickster that sometimes must be tricked or circumvented.
- Train by using meditation to reach the Stillpoint.

Internet key words: *tonal, nagual, Toltec teaching; Coyote, Rabbit, Trickster; shadow self; meditation techniques*

Chapter Two

Creating Sacred Spaces in Nature

*The power of the world always works in circles,
and everything tries to be round.*

—BLACK ELK
OGLALA SIOUX, 1863–1950

Just as there is sacred space within us from which to do ceremony, there can be sacred space around us within which to do ceremony. And just as we must have an internal framework to do ceremony—discerning our authentic self from ego and personality—so we must have an external framework for the Powers of earth and sky to help us do ceremony. The most effective external framework is an understanding of the world in terms of a medicine wheel, which according to Native American tradition is a physical manifestation of spiritual energy, showing how the power of the world works in circles.

Understanding the Medicine Wheel of the World

Interestingly, today some of the most ancient indigenous concepts of cosmology are finding expression in the most advanced notions of how the universe originated and operates—ideas that are at the heart of sacred ceremony.

Physicists tell us that the universe is round so that if we had a magic gun capable of shooting a bullet straight out into space, eventually it would return to us. Native people have known for millennia how energy and power work in circles, a notion eloquently expressed by Black Elk, an Oglala Sioux holy man.[1] As he has noted, all things in nature try to be round, from the smallest, the nest of the hummingbird, to the most powerful, the hurricane. The Earth is round and the seasons are round, just as the universe, scientists now tell us, is round, too. Within this infinite, round universe, the Creator created for us a beautiful three-dimensional circle, the Earth, that more properly could be called the Earth Mother, since she gives us life and all things with which to live. On the Earth Mother, everything in nature is round like her. The seasons and days are cyclical, and forms are circular. If we forget this, we have only to look above and see the round sun and moon and distant stars, all of which appear to circle us. So too is a person's life cyclical, from the baby's morning of life and youth's midday of life to the adult's evening and night before sleep and reawakening. Thus, everything in nature tends to move by cyclical forces and have circular forms, as well as being interconnected in what is called the sacred hoop of life, or the medicine wheel of the world.

In addition to the cyclical forces and circular forms of nature, all things on this Earth Mother have their own inherent power, their own "medicine," which can be for good or ill depending on how it is expressed in each moment. Just as the white light of a crystal encompasses various colors that can be seen when we shift it, all things have their own "medicine" or energy that makes them appear to have a certain effect and is a "color" of the Creator's white light. In doing ceremony, we want the good medicine, which in Cherokee is called the nvwati, to become activated, which is why we create the medicine wheel of the world as a framework within the material plane in which we live.

To find sanctuary and create sacred spaces for ceremony, it is essential to understand the "language" of the world, the origin of the energy that comprises the world, how it manifests as form, and how it can be employed in ceremony. In the beginning, the Creator created a single point, one that was round and contained the potential for all things. The creation of this point also gave rise to movement, called the flow of creation. All things have the potential qualities of motion and stasis or rest, such as the heart, for example.

Since the single point had within and around it the potential for all things, it existed multidimensionally. Two-dimensionally, this point was a circle; and seen from the side, a straight line; and, with the added quality of motion, it is a spiral. The spiral, which when seen two-dimensionally appears as a wave, incorporates within it the qualities of motion and stasis, polarity (male and female energies), and frequency (as all parts of the electromagnetic spectrum).

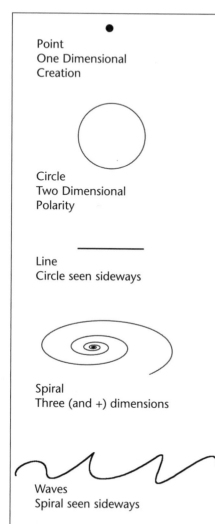

Point
One Dimensional
Creation

Circle
Two Dimensional
Polarity

Line
Circle seen sideways

Spiral
Three (and +) dimensions

Waves
Spiral seen sideways

From one dimension, a point, came creation; from two dimensions, polarity, come the circle, the straight line, the spiral, and the wave, expanding into three and more dimensions. This is the basis for all things in the world, what is really real, and the reality of nature, from its point of origin, explaining the flow of creation (from one to many; creation itself ongoing). The shapes, forms, and powers—the building blocks of sacred geometry—are at the heart of all healing medicine and all sacred ceremony. These shapes and forces comprise the medicine wheel of the world.

To understand how the energy that comprises everything interacts, it is important to realize that we each are oscillators of energy, whether we are conscious of it or not. Driven by the giant oscillator in our chests, our heart, which like a pendulum pumps energy in and out throughout our bodies, our chakras (a Sanskrit word meaning "wheels of light") constantly emit energy that transmits information regarding our health and our thoughts and feelings through various dimensions of time and space. Twice, when the heart is fully expanded, and when it is fully closed, there is one micro-millisecond in which perfect rest or stasis is achieved, and it is connected with everything; all is motion and rest. And just as we constantly send energy out into the universe, we continuously receive energy and can thus be affected by our environment, either unconsciously, such as by a crowd or certain room, or consciously, such as by meditating or using a drum to call in guides and spirits.

Our minds are like radios. We can let the dial spin arbitrarily and thus be dictated to by our environment or we can consciously tune in or tune out whatever influences we feel. Just as we select certain frequencies on the radio among the perhaps one thousand that are broadcast, we can choose what energies we allow to influence us by becoming more aware of the range and potential types of energy projected around us and learning to filter some types out while amplifying others.

Perceiving Broader Spectrums of the World

To gain increased awareness of the total spectrum of energies around us, it is necessary to learn to perceive beyond all that can be discerned by the physical senses. If we choose to see only with our physical eyes and hear with our physical ears, we miss most of what we are capable of perceiving and what the world has to offer. By opening our eyes to "nonordinary" reality and perceiving broader spectrums, we become capable of finding sanctuary and doing ceremony wherever we may be.

To achieve this ability, it is necessary to realize that everything we see around us in the material world is only a small part of what actually exists. From a broader perspective, all things exist in and come from a hidden order of the universe, which physicist David Bohm calls the implicate order, in contrast to the material world around us, or the explicate order.[2] To illustrate this principle, Bohm uses the example of what happens when ink is dropped into a beaker of swirling water. As it's diluted, the ink will form a line, representing the explicate order, that will disappear. If the water is then swirled in the opposite direction, the ink will reappear and return to its original position, following the same movements in reverse, exemplifying the implicate order. This illustrates how all things come from potential along lines that pre-exist and can go backwards and forwards in time into and out of existence. What is really real is this potential, the implicate order; what is manifested is the explicate order. In doing ceremony, we want to link up with the implicate order to create along the lines of our intent outcomes occurring in the explicate order.

Exposing Consensus Reality

To be able to distinguish between the explicate and implicate orders, we must first understand that the world we think we live in, the world as we perceive it to be, is not the real world but rather the consensus reality we share with others. For example, the world appears to be a flat surface, and yet we know it is round because we have been told it is so and have seen pictures from space. We think of the world as a stable place, but actually the world is spinning at thousands of miles per hour. Also this world we think is immovable is circling the sun at thousands of miles per hour, as well as the galaxy we call the Milky Way, and if it weren't for gravity we would be flung into the universe.

Further, we think of this world as solid, but every object is actually composed of more space than material substance. The distance between the center of an atom and its circling electrons is proportionate to that from the Earth to the sun. And matter itself is not very substantial. At its most basic, scientists say, matter is neither substance nor energy waves but qualities of both that "wink" in and out of existence. Some have called matter simply "frozen light" or light at a very low vibrational level. Thus the "things" we see around us— rocks, plants, animals, people—are actually all patterns of energy.

Not only is reality not what we perceive as real, but our physical perceptive abilities are also very limited. Our eyes see just a tiny sliver of the electromagnetic spectrum, and even then, they perceive only reflections. For example, our eyes register an orange as the color orange because orange light, rather than being absorbed by the fruit, reflects off of it. This reflected light is what reaches our eyes and is filtered through visual receptors before reaching the optic nerve, and the subjective interpretation of the brain. Anyone who has marveled at "optical illusions" knows that what we perceive with eye versus mind can be quite confusingly opposed.

Similarly, our ears pick up only a tiny fraction of the vibrations in our midst, while bats, for example, hear higher frequencies; our noses are not as sensitive as those of dogs; and our sense of touch is not as sophisticated as that of ants, with their antennae. Yet we insist that things only exist that can be seen, touched, heard, or smelled, and then only as we see, feel, hear, or smell them—that nothing else is real.

Limitations of Statistics and Probability

In addition to the fact that the consensus reality on which we depend is fundamentally flawed because of our limited physical sense ability and perception, we tend to base our views of the world and how it operates on statistics and probability. But using statistics is the easiest way to lie because statistics measure what has occurred in the past, and then only in a limited framework, and do not take into account what is occurring in the present or predict what will happen in the future. Probability is also flawed. For example, when flipping a coin, the probability it will land heads or tails seems to be 50–50, but the coin could also land on its rim. What if it does so twice in a row? It becomes the "random rat" and is excluded. The framework intervenes.

Politicians, journalists, and economists use such "lies" of statistics all the time. For example, if the stock market has gone down steadily for the past three months and a politician wants to make the incumbent look bad, he can use statistics to create a bar chart showing the stock market has dropped, say, 30 percent over the past three months. But if the framework were a year, it could be that rather than having dropped 30 percent, the stock market is actually 50 percent higher than a year ago and the 30 percent drop is actually only a slight downward "tick" on the graph. And if the framework is extended over twenty years, the bar graph would only show an upward trend, perhaps double or triple the values of the past.

Also, at any time something might happen that could result in a stock market crash, making all the statistics and probabilities meaningless, such as the Great Depression. Other ways statistics and probability can be affected are by observation and expectation. Physicists tell us that whenever an object is observed, the very act of observing changes the quality and behavior of that object. And if we expect something to happen, even if we express hope that it will not, such as in saying, "I hope that doesn't happen," our investment of energy in the event increases the probability it will occur.

The Transient Nature of Value

Ultimately, it is our belief system that attributes value to certain phenomena. For instance, economies depend on what people believe about their personal status and the state of the world. The concept of value, in most parts of the world, is based on money and, further, tied to the

U.S. dollar. The dollar is currently to a fairly large extent being propped up by the Chinese, who have pegged their yuan to it and are holding vast sums of U.S. dollars. But this could change rapidly if the Chinese decided the dollar had no value and dumped it all to buy gold; in response, investors around the world could suddenly decide that the Chinese were right and dump their dollars for gold; and insurance companies and pension funds could decide they'd better play it safe and dump their dollars for gold; and the central banks and governments, no matter how much they might protest, would be forced to dump their dollars for gold or they would be left holding worthless paper. Suddenly, despite the official stance of the world's governments, gold would be the standard. Everything of value based on money would be devalued, and we would have to return to another value as the framework for exchanging labor or goods such as chickens.

The world as we perceive it is created by where we focus our attention, and politicians, wanting our attention placed on material things, manipulate religious and spiritual principles to support these material goals. Further, wealth is defined by those who have it, and they ensure their own status by encouraging scarcity among others, who support the system because they want the status. This man-made view of the world based on scarcity and want is not the real world.

Advertising also functions to shape consensus reality and reinforces notions of value through association and imagery. That is why ads about products feature happy, healthy, successful, self-assured people with orderly lives. If people in ads drinking Fizz-Pop Soda look healthy, self-assured, and radiant with happy kids, people will want to buy Fizz-Pop Soda so they can be healthy, self-assured, and radiant, too, with kids who don't whine and never get dirty. And commercials for Shapely Hair Shampoo featuring attractive women in the shower imply that if individuals buy the product they too might enjoy sensual experiences. While our rational mind knows that such implications are ridiculous, our emotional self is often drawn to the false promises and idealized images. What such advertisers are selling is not soap but dreams; and ironically, they want to sell us on the outside qualities we already potentially have on the inside: happiness, self-confidence, sensuality. The moment we stop looking outside of ourselves to fill our perceived deficits (scarcity and want) and recognize the attributes we already have—such as an abundance of life and love all around us—the allure of scarcity will fade, along with the want for Fizz-Pop Soda or Shapely Hair Shampoo.

This human-oriented world is the one we focus on, respond to, live within, but it is not really real. It's an illusory reality. The physics of it, the geometry, is chaotic, limited, artificial, and has no essential structure behind it. It is the tonal and does not acknowledge the nagual, the possibilities for miracles as a constant, the unexplained. It is predictable, comfortable, and false; but few things are truly predictable or comfortable or enduring; the only constant is change.

If we base our reality on the outside world and what others tell us, we are as fractured, disjointed and divided as is this human-oriented world, and what we are told is "reality." If we base our world on nature, what's really real, its processes, its geometry, and its forces, with ourselves the center of this medicine wheel of the world, within the sacred circle of life, and an integral part of it, and being one with it, we are whole and complete. We find sanctuary in ourselves and our world.

Reality isn't what we think it is, yet that is precisely how we perceive it, that is, what we think it is; what we perceive and how we perceive forms, shapes and becomes our reality. This sacred circle of perception and acting upon it is how we find and maintain sanctuary, being one with nature. While the Creator creates abundance, humans create scarcity, fearful that only man-made things can fulfill our dreams. Fortunately, we can tap into limitless potential for abundance as soon as we realize that the power conveyed throughout consensus reality, the explicate order, is illusory. It's easy to lose ourselves in this illusory world and forget who we are and what is real. The only real power, that of the Creator, is conveyed through unseen forces of the implicate order, such as the medicine wheel of the world, which, by way of ceremony, offers all we could desire, when embraced, creating sanctuary within and without.

Harnessing the Power of the Medicine Wheel

Today's world is profuse with negative energy, the constant drumbeat of war and terror pounding like a giant fist that stretches the fabric of the Earth's substance. We can alter this situation by recognizing the medicine wheel of the world, the really real world, and accessing its power. You carry the medicine wheel of the world wherever you go. It is around you all the time, whether you recognize it or not, for you are the medicine wheel, the center from which all the directions derive. You are one with the universe, and your soul is its center.

Although calling it by various names, most indigenous cultures have recognized the power of the circle, the medicine wheel of the world. Its form can be seen at ancient ceremonial grounds in the Americas, Native American kivas in the American Southwest, and ancient megalithic stone circles scattered across each continent. It also appears in ancient Chinese mandalas of the Buddha-Land, which express in various ways the five elements (wood, fire, earth, metal, and water).[3] In addition, the Chinese used a Pa Gua, an eight-sided medicine wheel (representing the four directions plus those between them—southeast, southwest, northwest, northeast), as a meditative path to enlightenment.

Probably the most celebrated medicine wheel on earth is the megalithic stone circle of Stonehenge on the Salisbury Plain in England. Scientists call it an ancient calendar since its stones are aligned with astronomical bodies for observances of the seasons.

Certain shapes can be seen as representing time and events. A circle expresses the cycles of life. When the element of time is added to a circle, it becomes a spiral. Events are viewed as points in the circle, propelled by the flow of creation—the intent of the Creator—which is ongoing and infinite. The late Ian Xel Lungold, creator of the Mayan Calendar Conversion Codex showed how the circle with straight lines, expressed in the Mayan pyramids, describes time, space, and events.[4]

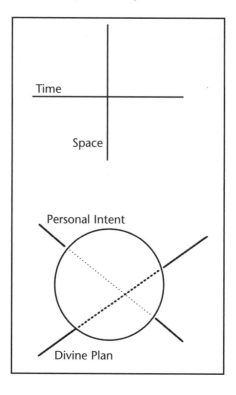

In these circular configurations, the location from which the universe was viewed determines how time and space are defined, while alternatives are excluded as being "unreal." For example, the Western Gregorian calendar is based on only the physical world—the world as seen from the Western perspective that regards only tangible events as real. If you made a cross with a perpendicular line representing time and a horizontal line representing space, you would have a calendar like ours that pinpoints particular dates around the globe. By contrast, the Mayans did not recognize physical reality as being as significant as Spirit and the destiny of individuals in the scheme of the divine. They perceived a world in which physical reality was a shadow of Spirit, a perspective that is reflected in their calendar. If we take the time/space cross of our modern calendar and put it in a circle (representing a sphere three-dimensionally), then draw one line (personal intent/personality) through it at one angle and another line (divine plan) through it at another angle, we have a more accurate, three-dimensional calendar, or medicine wheel that can function as a framework of the world for allowing us to do ceremony anywhere, anytime.

The more we learn of sacred geometry, the more sense we can make of this world we live in.[5] And embracing the concept of a medicine wheel of the world gives us a means for coordinating the sacred space within with the sacred space without, to evoke the good medicine in all things for healing.

Exercise 2 Welcoming the Powers of the Directions

While at the center of our medicine wheel of the world, which encircles and stretches as far as the eye can see, we find balance, peace, and power. The Diné (Navajo people) have a poignant expression for this state: walking in beauty. When we are at the center, walking in beauty, we invoke the four directions, or the four harmonies, which in Cherokee are called *unoli* (you-know-lee), literally "winds." They are great Powers. The following exercise provides a way to experience the center of your medicine wheel and, while welcoming the energies of the world by acknowledging and honoring the four directions, access power to do ceremony.

Stand someplace where there is a vista, or at least a sense of spaciousness. Turning to each of the directions, beginning with the east, acknowledge and honor its meaning according to its description below and invite its power into your medicine circle.

East: opening the eyes, being here now. Each day is unlike any other day, so when the sun rises in the morning, it offers a new beginning, a promise of potential. Within each day, every moment is unique and significant. In the words of a Sanskrit poem: Yesterday is just a memory, tomorrow is just a dream. The only time that matters is right now. All baggage of the past must be dropped for us to truly enjoy an experience of the present. If we are remembering events of the past or thinking about the future, we are not able to receive the power of being present. This *unoli* is red, a primal power. Invite this *unoli* into your circle and accept her gift. Thank this *unoli* for being here.

South: appreciating vigor, wholeness, healing. When the sun rises to its greatest height, we feel its power. This is the time of vigor, beauty, strength, and healing. Imagine a field of green corn growing beneath the golden sun high in the deep blue sky. The corn creaks as it grows, reaching for the golden light to find fulfillment, wholeness. All the while, its roots run deep in the soil, holding it earthbound as it draws food and water from the Earth Mother. We are the corn reaching for higher power, healing, and wholeness. By giving our energies and prayers to it, we receive its golden light, its healing and wholeness; in return, we offer our prayers, our spoken thoughts for others, and our gratitude. This *unoli* is golden, a light beyond our reach. Invite this *unoli* into your circle, and join with her, feeling her warming influence making you whole. Thank this *unoli* for being here.

West: setting sun, introspection, going within. When the sun sets, the earth is plunged into darkness, making it hard to find our way. We stumble about, blind and unknowing, as if trapped in the "dark night of the soul." Our tendency is to reject this darkness in ourselves and in others, to go blindly along, feeling lost and isolated, with questions yet no answers. But this darkness is vital for us and our world, since without it we could have no light. Light and dark are one for the Creator, who created them so we could see. Instead, we must see as the Creator sees, by looking within at the spark of the Creator to illuminate our way in the outside world. We cannot depend on outer things, but must walk as the Creator guides us, from within. This *unoli* is black and comes in many forms. Invite this *unoli* into your circle and join with her, feeling her urging you to look within. Thank this *unoli* for being here.

North: opening to cold, white light, higher power, ancestors, wisdom. In the darkest night, the stars wheel overhead, shining brightly as our dreams give landscape to our souls. This direction reflects higher wisdom, the white light of truth, the worlds outside our worlds, where we come from and where we will go, where the ancestors reside and where the children will come from, the source of light, of being. Sometimes the white light of truth is too great for our human eyes to bear; it blinds us, causing us to live in denial. We open our hearts and minds, and bare our souls to this power, giving ourselves compassion, so that we learn to live in truthful, loving ways with all beings, knowing we are one with them and allowing our steps to be guided by those who have gone before and those who are yet to come. We realize that what we know, and who we are, is very little. We allow our humility to open us to as much of the truth as we can stand, to help us on our way. This *unoli* is blinding white, so we can only see her shadow in this world, a rainbow of many colors. Invite this *unoli* into your circle and join with her, allowing her to give you insight, understanding, and guidance. Thank this *unoli* for being here.

Exercise 3 Using Divination to Connect Realms of Reality

Divination is an age-old practice that works because every mind has within it a Stillpoint, where past, present, and future exist simultaneously. Due to the sacred geometry of time, as a circle with lines intersecting, we are within a flow shared with all things. Normally, we derive meaning for the present from the past and it colors our view of the future. But past and future are only mental constructs we use to function with others, agreeing to what is the present, the past, and the future. Thus, in daily life the present is simply something we use to make sense of random activity in the past, in an attempt to bring order and predictable outcomes to the future. We are always at the Stillpoint, but our rational mind, our ego, will not accept the Stillpoint, for the mind then would have no function. Practicing divination is a good way to gain more inner knowledge of these concepts.

To use divination for connecting realms of reality, first find your sacred space within, the Stillpoint, then connect to the implicate order, from which everything in the explicate order derives—divination = divine-ation—through the aid of various tools. Tarot cards, runes, and the I Ching all assist in connecting with things in both the implicate and the explicate orders. Theoretically, anything can be used for divination, even the contents of a pocket or purse. All it takes is:

• A set, rigid grid of conscious intent

• Objects with set, understood meanings

• Randomness

When using the Tarot cards to read the past, present, and future, begin by setting your intent to place the cards, each of which has a set meaning, in the following order: past to the left, present in the middle, future to the right. With your eyes closed and your mind clear, practicing Stillpoint, shuffle the deck and lay out three cards as described. The cards will have meaning within the context of your intent. When working with runes, shuffle the bag and, practicing Stillpoint, choose three runes at random, setting them down as described. The runes will tell the past, present, and future conditions. The I Ching is a bit trickier, because there are more combinations, resulting in greater precision but requiring skill to interpret.

The same principle applies to any set of objects, no matter how common. By giving them meanings and an assigned order, then casting them randomly using the Stillpoint to guide your actions, they will give a message for the moment.

If you develop stillness, circumventing the ego or distracting it by focusing on nonthought, the rest of your mind can perceive the implicate order. Then the alignment of the moon, sun, and stars with the planet, the inhalation and exhalation of the earth itself, a flight of birds, a single movement of a breath, the fleeting shadow of a thought, all become one thing, and the world itself becomes divinatory.

From the Energy Notebook: Respecting the Use of Power

When doing ceremony or practicing any type of energy medicine for healing or help, remember that you are dealing with powers of the universe, forces of earth and sky. Because you are channeling these tremendous powers, you must always respect them and know how to handle them.

Many people find early on that energy will manifest outside themselves in powerful ways. They might burn up their computers while writing; objects could fall off shelves in stores where they are shopping; when they enter a room, the lights might flicker or light bulbs burn out. Some are amazed and think, "What power I have!" and even encourage it. But such an attitude, the mark of a rank novice, is misguided, thoughtless, and dangerous. "Personal power" is not personal, and should not be used for ostentatious displays—certainly not ones that are out of control—but in precisely guiding energy to do as appropriate.

Energy comes from the heart (not the mind), from the Creator (not the ego), and it can only be seen in its totality (not in single manifestations).

For example, a young man called me a few years ago and left the following message on my answering machine: "I've decided you're my teacher." Days later, he showed up at my door. His mind was full of ideas about the components of energy work, and he seemed to think that if he just pushed the right button, I would "dispense" information like soda from a vending machine, whereupon he could go merrily on his way, full of knowledge.

I told him repeatedly that knowledge of this sort takes time—that it is not gleaned intellectually but rather through experience. I explained that knowledge is found not by repeating the ideas of others but by drawing ideas into the heart and mind and acting on them until they become one's own way. And although a teacher can provide direction, what is taught is not the ideas per se but the guidance for finding one's own answers.

I invited the young man to come sweat with me at the Bear Lodge (Asi/Inipi) and told him the ceremony would take all day. We live surrounded by about 50,000 acres of national forest, and the lodge is deep in the woods about a mile away, accessible by a four-wheel-drive vehicle. Because the young man was extremely inquisitive, I invited my friend Boe Many Knives Glasschild, a Choctaw shaman who is given to long, philosophical conversations, figuring he could answer all the questions. But once we arrived at the lodge and built the sacred fire, the young man became incessantly inquisitive and Boe remained utterly mum, enjoying the experience of watching me squirm. I kept telling the young man to simply watch what we did, feel the energy of it, and we could discuss it later; however, he chattered on about the 200 or so names for God. Impatiently, I motioned at the sacred fire and said, "All you need to know is right here!" And the fire, responding, shot up into a flame twelve feet high. Boe and I, taken aback, just looked at each other. After a few moments of silence, with his eyes big as dinner plates, the young man said he had to go to work that afternoon, so I drove him back to the house. As we pulled up, he jumped out of the truck so fast he ran barefoot to his car and sped away leaving his sandals behind.

The lesson was that you cannot make rational sense of energy work. You have to be literally "out of your mind" to do this type of work. If you try to rationalize it, your mind will get so full that your heart won't be able to express itself and your soul won't be able to make the work meaningful.

A further reminder for me was that ostentatious displays of power show a failure of mastery, in this case my impatience mirroring the young man's impatience.

Review

How to create sacred spaces in nature:

- Recognize that the world is a sacred circle, or medicine wheel.
- Recognize that you have a place within the sacred circle of the world, and the world reflects what you think of it.
- Recognize that all is one within the medicine wheel of the world.
- Welcome the powers of the directions and learn from them, being careful what you evoke.

Internet key words: *Sacred geometry, medicine wheel, sweat lodge, Asi/Inipi*

Chapter Three

Learning to Make Ceremonies Effective

*The Tree of Peace has four white roots
extending to Earth's four corners.
Anyone who desires peace can follow the roots to
their source and find shelter under The Great Tree.*

—DEGANAWIDA (THE PEACEMAKER)

Ceremony is what happens or is created; ritual is what helps it happen; and intent turns ritual into ceremony. For example, when one enters a church and feels the presence of God, it is not the pews, stained glass, or pulpit—the props—that give that feeling but the spirit of the place created by the prayers or intent (energy) of the people who have been there and connected to Spirit. The props are there to remind people why they have come.

Similarly, when one finds solace, healing, or forgiveness in a church service, it is not because of the songs, words, sequence of events, or rituals—but because of the intent (energy) of the people in attendance who allow themselves to experience solace, healing, or forgiveness, or give it to others. The rituals merely facilitate the expression and acceptance of that energy.

For example, at weddings, no matter how traditional or elaborate the attire, the cake, or the rituals performed, the most lasting impression is not of the bride's gown, the food, the music, or who caught the bouquet, but of the intent that turns the rituals into ceremony. In this case, the intent would be the love expressed during the event and in the invisible bond, which hopefully endures. In effect, every ceremony is a wedding—a joining of the highest intents of the individuals with the flow of creation, to achieve solace, healing, forgiveness, compassion, or wholeness.

Doing Ceremony with Power

To do ceremony with power, it is necessary first to create your sacred space, your "church," through intent and ritual. Such sacred space always exists in the implicate order and must be brought into the explicate order.

Objects and rituals can then be used to amplify your ability to touch the divine within and without and focus intent on the purpose of the ceremony. For example, in modern Christian churches, the lighting of candles, the waving of the salter's incense, and the singing are done not only because the candles are pretty, the scent sweet, or the songs beautiful, but also to bring the worshippers' intent to a point at which it can draw the beings present fully into the moment, ready to experience the eternal now, where power resides. During such rituals, worshippers know to cease internal dialogue, connect with the Stillpoint, and focus on the sacred moment so their state of mind is prepared for inner discovery and spiritual truth. The same is true of the use of objects and rituals in many other religious traditions, including Islamic, Jewish, Buddhist, and Native American. The holy man or woman creates an atmosphere of spiritual potential as surely as a craftsman builds a chair. The outcome depends entirely on the individuals present—their beliefs, expectations, and intentions.

For the seeker whose intent is to go beyond the confines imposed by expectations (prejudgments or consensus reality), it is essential to have total awareness of the moment, having suspended the tonal and given consciousness room for the nagual to emerge. This openness, which allows the divine to be expressed through the "hollow bone" of the seeker immersed in ceremony, is considered the most *waken* (wah-KAHN), the Lakota word for sacred. Becoming hollow to allow the Creator's power to come through involves appreciating and allowing all the powers—guides, angels, power animals, goddesses, spirit beings—to join and participate in creating miracles. The proper attitude is to humble ourselves before them, however small or seemingly inconsequential these powers may appear to us. It is this attitude of humility and openness that helps bring the divine powers into the human spirit, allowing them to manifest on this plane.

Power is generated when you are one with the essence of a thing and identify not with rational thought or self-image but with nonlinear time and place, the nagual becomes an integral part of your ceremony. And while medicine people can perform many acts that defy science, to them it's not the miracles themselves that count but the benefit they bring to the people and the fact that they could only be accomplished with right thinking, which involves becoming one with all beings and things, in what we might call the tree of life.

Developing Right Thinking

About one thousand years ago, a man called Deganawida (The Peacemaker) came among the Iroquois (Haudenosaunee) and taught the people a new way of thinking. Although born a Huron, he brought peace to the Mohawk, Oneida, Onondaga, Cayuga, and Seneca nations by teaching the Great Law of Peace, or way of right thinking, under what came to be known as the Iroquois Confederacy. This confederacy later formed the basis of the democracy the first colonists in America emulated, however imperfectly. The Great Law of Peace envisioned all men and women existing as equals, within one circle beneath the Great Tree of Peace, whose roots extended to the four cardinal directions and whose branches held an eagle that could see far into the future and warn of trouble. This image reflects the essence of right relations between all peoples.

When we develop right thinking, we become one with the tree of life, relating to all beings as leaves on this tree, our roots going deep within the earth, to all four directions, our limbs reaching to the sky, toward the Creator, our consciousness like the eagle with awareness of everything above and below, past and future. We are the Tree and we are the Eagle, as one. In this sacred space, we become one with everything and ultimately with the Creator.

Various cultures have names of their own for the Creator or for the sacred space where an individual is one with the Creator. In Sanskrit, the word for "sacred space" or "sacred altar" is yoni, which is also the name for the vagina, the place of birth. In ancient Hebrew, the name for the Creator is the initials of the four elements—fire, water, earth, and air—the basis of all things on earth: IHVH, or Yehovah. Among Native Americans, there are many names for the Creator, including the Great Mystery, the Center of All Things, the Great Spirit, and in Cherokee, *u halo tega* (the Source of All Power), *Ona*, or *Yowah*. The words *yoni*, ee-oh-vah, *ona*, and *yowah* share an intriguing similarity when spoken aloud.

Whatever name you choose to call the sacred space you create, realize that it has great power and when spoken aloud becomes an influential force in this world. It has power, however, only when spoken from the heart. Simply reciting words in rituals without the heart's intent is to revert to dogma that has no power. To speak with your heart and mind as one and to then act upon these words carries a certainty of faith that evokes the Powers of the Universe.

In effect, bringing right thinking to ceremony involves going deep inside the self in order to reach up to the Creator. So, just as the tree of life has not only high branches but also deep roots, go deep to reach high. And the deeper you go, the higher you can go.

Using right thinking to create sacred space and carry it with you wherever you go, thus being prepared to do ceremony, is like a spiritual journey. Hindus who go on pilgrimages call the sites they visit *tirthas*, a Sanskrit word meaning places where heaven and earth meet. Such pilgrimages are usually to a location where some great event has occurred or a god or goddess has been known to dwell. In the sacred space that you carry, the great event is your awareness of the world around you. It is awareness of sacred space, and the intent to enliven it with the Powers, that creates ceremony.

Individuals with such awareness and intent can tap this unlimited energy. Indigenous peoples throughout history sought "thin" places on the Earth where good energy was most intense and built medicine wheels or other monuments of earth or stone. Such places are *lela waken* (Lakota for very sacred), portals of power where the soul can be transported and ceremonies can be performed most effectively, by creating a sacred circle, inviting in the powers, and transforming the space through prayer.

Prayer is a dance between a person's consciousness and the divine. When you pray, your intents are focused, reinforced by the power of ritual, which provides a framework for manifestation. However large or small the ceremony, the implications of this dance are vast—your partner is eternal, the dance timeless, as your intent spirals forward and backward in time. Your intent, your spoken words in prayer, should be an affirmation because the Heavenly Father hears these words and the Earth Mother brings forth blooms wherever seeds are sown. With your intent heard and nurtured in this way, Spirit can then carry it out.

How to Pray

Prayer is not asking but affirming that the desired outcome is already present and allowing it to be manifested from the implicate to the explicate order. The desired outcomes of prayer must also be consistent with thoughts and actions. Most people don't realize that prayer consists not only of specific thoughts and actions but of all thoughts and actions, both personal and collective. No matter how powerful your intent or sacred ceremony might be, your prayer may be negated if your thoughts and actions contradict it. For example, if you pray for happiness and serenity but are often negative and prone to conflict, it's not likely what you pray for will come to pass, because it's been canceled out by the ongoing "prayer" of your existence. Nor can you put your hands together and say, "I want a Mercedes Benz," and expect to get one while your daily thoughts and actions fail to support such an outcome. It's true that when you pray in a sacred manner, focusing ritual and intent, that even one micro-millisecond of connection with the Divine could actually cause a Mercedes to manifest, since possibility is infinite. The Creator, however, knowing what is best for the flow of creation and what you are capable of handling, provides accordingly.

Your prayers must also affirm and acknowledge that the hoped-for events have already happened. And in a sense they have, with prayer inviting them into being here and now, assuming the Creator favors such outcomes. It's important to remember that things are meant to occur for the highest good for all, including plants, animals, and spirit beings.

Further, it is necessary to pay careful attention to the wording of your prayers. For example, if you say, "I want a Mercedes Benz" this prayer will likely be answered: you will want a Mercedes Benz. But you are not likely to get a Mercedes Benz, because you gave power to wanting it, not having it.

Prayers must have good intent as well, so that only the highest expression of the desire is manifested, without in any way limiting the good medicine provided. Indeed, in prayer we surrender to the greatest potential good, recognizing it has already happened and is only up to us to perceive it, thereby allowing it to become manifest. Our prayers have power when they flow with the flow of creation, which is considered the easiest path toward goodness.

Because prayers have power, it is wise not only to have good intent but to refuse to ask what went wrong if a particular prayer was not answered. For example, if your neighbor gets the Mercedes Benz, it is likely that your prayer for it was not aligned with the flow of creation. You cannot limit the Creator by imposing your own expectations; in fact, attempting to channel God into fulfilling the needs of your ego or personality may only create more disharmony, scarcity, and want, as that is the space from which the prayer originated. The Creator's creation manifests in unimaginably good ways because it is an eternal view encompassing the past, present, and future as one. It is not limited by our fickle expectations, but when we align with it, we may manifest beyond our wildest dreams.

So, to have effective prayers we want to pray from the heart, in the spirit of peace, love, compassion, light, healing, and growth, using the type of thinking that is not invested in outcome, allowing for manifestations that help the greatest number of beings. This is right-brain thinking. By contrast, if we use left-brain thinking, which is rational, we are not fully utilizing the power of prayer; the intent, now linear, can be diverted or subverted. Both left-brain and right-brain activity work in creating reality. The left brain thinks practically and is used to build roads, bridges, and skyscrapers. The right brain thinks holistically and functions in symbols and subtle shades of meaning that are appropriate for prayer. When we are in this state, our authentic self can be seen as a source of unlimited goodness and power, along with everyone we know and everything around us. For example, when medicine men perform prayers or ceremony to make rain, they are not praying for rain. They become one with Earth and sky and feel the need for rain, allowing for the possibility of it to happen, and with this window of belief, which is good for all beings, it can occur.

Finally, prayers should include thanks to all the spirit beings for their provisions and guidance, since the Powers cause miracles to occur. For example, you might end a prayer with the following words of gratitude:

Dear Lord, Creator, Earth Mother, Heavenly Father, Guides, Angels, Power Animals, and all Good Spirits—We thank you for allowing us to have ceremony and be here with you today; we are grateful for all things, and for all beings, so that we may be one with you. We thank you, Creator, for providing power, and light, and healing; we thank you, Earth Mother, for providing the food we eat, the air we breathe, all the things we need for life; we thank you, guides, for speaking so that we might hear you and follow your guidance; we thank you, power animals, for your protection and connection to all things; angels, we thank you for the miracles all around us, all the time, shifting the world so subtly and powerfully that we are hardly mindful of it; we thank you, goddesses of earth and sky, for the many miracles you perform in compassion, love, forgiveness, guidance, and healing; ancestors and good spirits, we thank you for watching over us, informing us and helping us act in a good way for all beings; we thank you for helping us to heal and bring balance, wholeness, and unity so that all may benefit; we thank you for accepting these words, this voice we send, in the good way it is intended, and thank you for correcting any mistakes or omissions we may make; we thank you for this day, this moment, this sharing. All our relations. Mitakuye Oyasin. Gus dii dada dv ni. *Amen.*

When we are one with the tree of life, we are connected with every living thing, and in the native tradition, every thing is alive, and has its own power, its good medicine: the *nvwati*. A native saying goes, the leaves of a single tree never make war against the others. When we become one with the tree of life, every being is our relation; we are all one, but diverse in how we appear in the world, but all connected by the single trunk and limbs of the tree of life. This is how miracles occur. In seeing our oneness, we may influence anything anywhere. We are all related; we are all connected. This is what is meant by the prayer, blessing, and injunction *mitakuye oyasin*, all our relations, in Lakota, or *gus dii dada dv ni* in Cherokee. In sacred geometry, once again, we become one with the sacred hoop of life, the great circle of all beings that is within the sacred great circle of the Earthly Mother. In Western thought, we see things rationally; that is, in a straight line; in the native way, we see things as circular, all points belonging to (related to) the same thing. In the Western way, time itself is seen as a straight line, sequentially, 1-2-3-4 . . . from point to point. But in native way, each moment is timeless; it has its own time, its own sequence. The basis of all energy medicine, and hence, what's really real, is that time is timeless because it's a circle, a spiral that comes from timelessness and into timelessness, winking into this reality as manifestation. In fact, each moment is timeless; each moment may be seen not as a straight line, but as a "V," going deeper into each moment, if total attention is given to it. Each moment, in ceremony, in the tree of life, is all time-no time, where the past and future are one with the present. This oneness is what is meant by being one with the tree of life. All is one in all its diversity and all its manifestations; within each moment is the infinite possibilities of miracles.

Exercise 4 Creating a Sacred Circle

Creating a sacred circle is a very important aspect of increasing the effectiveness of a ceremony, since it focuses your energies, leads to right thinking, and sets intent. Choose a place of power, a location in nature that is secluded or with a vista that "feels right," where your energies are most conducive to the sacred geometry of the land forms.[1] Walk straight out from this place to the east, about ten feet, or however large you want your sacred circle to be, then walk clockwise, stopping at each cardinal direction to feel the energies. Walk around this circle four times, each time singing or praying in thanks to the Creator and all beings for having this opportunity to share body, mind, heart, and soul, and sprinkling tobacco or cornmeal to form the perimeter of the circle. On the first round, you may wish to shake a rattle to break up the energies that are there, so they may conform to your sacred intent. Then, on the last round, light sage or cedar and walk clockwise in a spiral toward the center, waving the smoke to fill the circle. Afterwards, do as you are guided, performing the desired ceremony, or if you prefer, meditating or simply enjoying the sanctuary of nature.

Exercise 5 Healing with Spiral Energy

Wherever there is trauma, whether to humans or the earth, spiral energy radiates outward from it. A simple way to help alleviate the trauma is to get a spiral of energy flowing in the opposite direction, in resistance to the spiral produced by the trauma. For example, if you accidentally burn or cut a finger, immediately hold the unhurt hand about eight inches over the injury with your palm open to sense whether the spiral of energy is emanating clockwise or counterclockwise from the injury. If it is clockwise, slowly turn your open palm counterclockwise, winding it gradually back and forth like a clock, all the while pushing your palm against the spiral emanating from the injury. If you feel no resistance, try turning your open hand in the other direction. Once you feel resistance, continue turning your palm in that direction until you no longer feel the opposition. Whenever there is trauma, applying resistance by activating healing energy in the opposite direction should lessen the pain and hasten healing.[2]

Exercise 6 Checking In with Your Inherent Wisdom

Using kinesiology, it is possible to check in with inherent wisdom to determine if a proposed course of action is advisable. First, set a standard, or baseline, from which to make positive or negative assessments. To set a baseline, hold your right hand on your abdomen (the *hara*), clear your mind, and ask a question to which you know the answer, such as: "My name is (your name)?" Then see if your right hand moves to the left or right, which will be the standard by which to assess other answers, although you can "reset" the standard at any time by changing intent. Use this system at any time to see what your highest self connected with Spirit would advise in response to questions you ask. This system works only with questions that can be answered "yes" or "no." Also, the guides and angels have no concept of time, so don't ask, "Will this be soon?" "Soon" could be an eon. Rather, ask "One hour?" "Two hours?" Remember too that conditions can change, since we live along time lines that are variable.

Exercise 7 Connecting with the Tree of Life Within

The following meditation, which takes only about thirty minutes, can help you find the tree of life within you, so you can "go there" whenever you desire. Have a friend read it to you, or record it and play it back so that during the meditation you will be free to connect with the power within you, see the particular energies in nature, and become one with them.[3]

With your eyes gently closed, take a few deep breaths. Imagine that you can breathe out the tensions in your body and breathe in the beautiful energy all around you.

Let each breath take you deeper and deeper into a state of relaxation.

(Pause for fifteen seconds to allow the breath to relax the body.)

Now relax all your muscles, releasing any tension in them one by one, as follows. In sequence, relax the muscles of your neck and shoulders, your arms, upper and lower back, stomach and abdomen, legs and feet, so that your entire body is in a state of peace.

Visualize a radiant light of any color above your head. Allowing this light to deepen your level of attention, let it flow down into your body through the top of your head, illuminating every cell with peace and healing.

Counting backwards from ten to one, let each number take you deeper into the relaxed state.

Ten … nine … eight … deeper and deeper you go …

Seven … six … five … more and more peaceful and relaxed …

Four … three … two … one … so calm and serene …

In this wonderful state of peace and tranquility, imagine yourself walking down a beautiful path in a quiet meadow aware of the beautiful flowers and the warming sun calming you, healing you.

Up ahead, you see the path crossing a fresh stream shaded by tall trees. Follow the path to the babbling stream.

Rocks in the shallow water of the stream form a perfect footpath. Step gently on them and go past the big one in the middle to get to the other side.

On reaching the other side you see an inviting open forest teeming with trees of all kinds and light, since it is only slightly shaded from the sun. Follow the path into the forest, noticing how large the grasses and ferns are, how softly your feet tread on the damp leaves, and how pungent the air is, alive with wonderful smells of vegetation.

Continue following the path until you see a large, tall tree with which you feel a special connection. Notice every feature of this tree—its width, height, the feeling of its bark.

(Pause for fifteen seconds.)

Put your arms around the tree, as far as you can reach.

Feel the bark against your cheek. Smell its fragrance. Experience how rooted in the earth the tree is and how alive it feels.

Feel yourself walking into the tree, merging with it. Feel your feet going down into the earth, past hundreds of roots, until your toes touch a crystal cave, and healing light, coursing up through them, enters the rest of your body.

Feel the light flowing into your heart and through your arms and legs.

Feel rooted, alive, and flooded with light and energy.

(Pause for fifteen seconds.)

Feel this energy carrying you upward through the crown of your head.

Feel your arms, as branches of the tree, stretching out in the sunshine over the forest.

Feel your fingers, as leaves, enjoying the life-giving rays of the sun, and draw into yourself the energies of everything around you, all of which meet in your heart.

(Pause for fifteen seconds.)

You are one with the tree.

Your roots are deep, deep, deep within the moist earth.

Your toes are in the crystal cave.

Your body is the tree, tall and strong, able to withstand any wind or rain element of the earth.

You are one with all the power of the earth and sky.

Your awareness is able to extend as far as you wish, over all the land.

You are centered in your heart, with life-giving, healing energy from the earth and sky meeting there. What do you see? What is before you? What is behind you? What insights do you have?

(Pause for thirty seconds.)

To return to full waking consciousness, count from one to ten, letting each number increasingly awaken you. At the count of ten open your eyes and notice how wide awake and alert you are, in full control of both body and mind.

Now, write down what you saw and felt, and what messages you received during the meditation.

From the Energy Notebook:
Be Careful What You Pray for!

We must recognize that our thoughts and words have power and that doing ceremony magnifies that power. When in the sacred circle of ceremony, all our thoughts and actions are prayers evoking the implicate order into the explicate order, or manifesting the visible from the world of the invisible. Therefore, be careful what you "pray" for with your thoughts and words, as they can cause unwanted things to manifest.

I was reminded of the power of thoughts and words when my wife Annette and I were preparing to do a sweat with visiting friends, at our Bear Lodge, which is dedicated to the bear. Bear energy is healing, as reflected in the medicine bear fetishes often seen with a lightening bolt painted or carved on its body, symbolizing this power, which relates to going within to heal.

We were sitting outside the lodge while the grandfathers (stones) were heating in the sacred fire, and the conversation turned to snakes. Annette and I have no particular affinity or aversion to snakes; but our friends had a fear of snakes and told many scary stories about snake encounters. After a while, I began to feel uneasy and suggested that since we were sitting in the sacred circle of the lodge, perhaps we should change the subject. Then an owl hooted, signifying that the grandfathers were ready, so we did our sweat.

A few days later, Annette and I decided to have a "family sweat," something we do often, to pray together and purify body, mind, heart, and soul for healing and finding guidance. As the first round started, and I was pouring water inviting the good spirits in and thanking our power animals for acting as gatekeepers to ward off negative energies, we both heard a loud pop and then a thump. Now, it's not uncommon for spirits to appear in the lodge—sometimes as bright lights, faces, or spirit animals—but Annette said in an ominous tone, "I think a snake just appeared. It's huge." There was a pause of about the time it takes to blink twice, then she was out the door, with light flooding in. There, coiled on the west side of the lodge (the place of honor and direction of the bear) was a large, five-foot King snake. "I guess that ends round one," I said.

With a stick, we held open the canvas lodge wall, and the snake slithered out and calmly headed toward the woods. We resumed our ceremony and I prayed, "Thank you, Creator, for this wonderful guest—and reminder to watch what we say inside our sacred circle at the lodge."

Review

How to make ceremonies effective:

- Recognizing that everything is related, connect with the tree of life.
- Develop right thinking.
- Create a sacred circle unifying everything in the world.
- Learn how to pray.
- Allow the powers to make whole and manifest that which needs manifesting.
- Consistently thank the powers and the Creator.

Internet keywords: *wakan, lela wakan, Deganawida, the tree of life*

Chapter Four

Performing Ceremonies for Self-Discovery and Healing

*The survival of the world depends on
our sharing what we have, and working together.
If we do not, the whole world will die.
First the planet, and next the people.*

—Frank Fools Crow, Lakota Medicine Man

All ceremonies open with consecration of a circle, the center of which represents sacredness and simultaneously allows the person doing ceremony to access the Stillpoint within so the sacred space within and without are experienced as connected. After this, every ceremony follows the same basic structure: it honors the directions in prayers of thanksgiving and gratitude for all; continues as a living prayer through thoughts, thanks, pleas, and rituals; and ends with a prayer of gratitude for all that has happened before, during, and after the ritual.

The ceremonies described in this chapter focus on the outcomes of self-discovery and healing. Good preparation for doing most of them involves learning how to create and use a medicine wheel. The wheel itself is less important than the space within; the wheel is a representation and reminder of the oneness and diversity of all life; it is a framework for doing ceremony, creating an outward sacred space to reflect the inner sacred space, and is an ancient practice known throughout all cultures in various forms across the globe. Within this circle, in this female principle of the vessel or contained space, your mind, heart, and soul become one with Creator to manifest in the world.

Exercise 8 Making a Medicine Wheel for Doing Ceremony

To experience connectedness to everything, and thus oneness with the world, make a medicine wheel. This is something you can do anywhere, anytime, indoors or out, in a backyard or in the farthest outback.

Many types of medicine wheels can be made to accomplish various purposes, but the one described here is the medicine wheel of the world, which helps establish a framework for doing ceremony. First, create a sacred circle; it can be as small as an altar on a desktop or as large as a huge ring on the ground outdoors in the landscape. Next, find five small stones and place one in the center of the circle, then position each of the others in one of the four directions—east, south, west, and north. (If you wish, gather four more stones and place them at the midpoints to represent southeast, southwest, northwest, and northeast.)

Looking at the configuration you have mapped out, recognize that medicine wheels have six primary directions: above, below, and each of the four cardinal directions. There is a seventh point, the center, which is also the seat of the soul, where we join with the Creator. The above place is where the male force of Spirit resides, while the below place is where the Earth Mother is located. Between those points we walk, flanked by the worlds of earth and sky—our flesh of the earth, our spirits the sparks of Spirit.

Each of the four directions is a power and is ascribed one of the colors of the four races of human beings: red, yellow, black, and white. We recognize these powers as:

East (red): Dawn, beginnings, new awareness

South (yellow): Youth, growing, vigor, healing

West (black): Inner vision, reflection, endings

North (white): Wisdom of ancestors, higher power, guidance

Just as each direction has its power, so does each day have its own energy (red, yellow, black, or white), and the days occur in cycles of thirteen as well as in hours and minutes. So, the configuration you have created for your medicine wheel represents time and space—in short, the world itself.

As you have placed a stone at each of the four directions, notice that what appeared first to be a square is actually a circle. You could place stones outward from the center indefinitely, and it would be a stone circle, which is what the Hopi and the ancient Celts use as sanctuaries for prayer and healing ceremonies. Similarly, within the circle you have constructed you can do ceremony. Invite the powers in and say your prayers, which go out to the universe.

The power of the medicine wheel emanates from the sacred geometry of the shapes and their interrelationships. The basis of sacred geometry is reflected in the fact that all forms on the Earth Mother are composed of the circle and the straight line. The circle is female energy, which is inclusive; the straight lines radiating out from the center are male energy, which divides. From the moment of creation, there was a circle, the dot that includes all; and from that circle came the straight line, which divided. It is the nature of the world that the male and female energies join to generate all forms. In ceremonies of all kinds, we want to recognize and allow these forces to create what is best for us each individually and for all beings.

To do ceremony, or initiate a dialogue between the sacred space within and without, we must become one with the energy of the central point in the medicine wheel and the Stillpoint in us. The feeling of being one with Spirit is a soul connection we carry from lifetime to lifetime like the air hoses of underwater divers that connect them to their energy source above the surface. Also like divers, our "diving suits," our bodies, are removable and inter-changeable. We think we live in these particular "diving suits" and that our surroundings are real, but they are actually a dream of the world. And beyond this dream, we each have the power of the Creator within us, which is the power we access in prayer. As such, whoever we are and wherever we are, we are important instruments of the Creator. By giving prayers in the medicine wheel, at the heart of the flow of creation, we use its power to help bring balance to the world.

Fire, Water, Earth, and Air

From time immemorial, the essential elements of life have been described as fire, water, earth, and air. (In Chinese tradition, there are five elements-wood, fire, earth, metal, and water.) In all wisdom traditions, these elements have been considered sacred and powerful. It is therefore no coincidence that they have been used symbolically in religious traditions and ceremonies, and appear in sacred doctrines around the world. This is not only because they comprise the essence of life on the planet but also because they are associated with the mystery of transmutation. When something is burned in fire, its form is changed and the smoke goes heavenward. When something is placed in water, it is altered so that it may merge again with life. When something is buried in the earth, it returns to the substance from whence it came. When something is left out in nature, it is transformed by air and weather elements. Each of these transmutation processes leads back to the Earth Mother and Heavenly Father, and can be used in sacred ceremony to provide for self-discovery and healing. Moreover, each of these elements are a Power themselves; they hold qualities that extend beyond the immediate. When we work with these elements in ceremony, we honor the medicine each holds intrinsically to alter reality itself.

Fire

In ancient lore, the gift of fire from a god or sacred being is often depicted as a turning point in the development of humans—from Prometheus bringing fire to the people in Western mythology to Spider giving fire to the people in Native stories. The momentous change in humans results in part because fire is crucial for survival and also because it has great power that can be used for good or ill—and thus presents us with moral dilemmas. Ordinary fires, the product of will, are used for mundane purposes; sacred fires, the product of spiritual intent, are used for ceremony. In ceremony, a fire is made so participants can experience it as a sacred thing, in contrast to a fire for cooking or for sheer enjoyment. We perceive fire as light and heat, but sacred fire has the power of the Creator within it and is therefore a portal for sacrificial giving and receiving. Sacred fire also is prepared in a reverent manner with carefully selected woods and tended during ceremony with honor and respect, as if it were a participant. And when the ceremony is finished, it is allowed to expire naturally, rather than being artificially extinguished.

Sacred fire is so important in Native American cultures that special individuals are often trained to be in charge of it. For example, among the Cherokee, who are sometimes called the People of the Fire, a person is designated the firekeeper and is trained a decade or more before taking on this holy position.

These ways have been handed down orally for thousands of years. In addition to the knowledge of sacred fire derived from the ancestors, the fires themselves come from the coals and ashes of ancestors, having been constantly tended as eternal flame.

As fuel for sacred fires, Native American cultures use woods they most revere. The Cherokee, for instance, use primarily seven such woods—white pine, white cedar, black cherry, sycamore, hickory, cottonwood, and walnut. It is because the standing ones (trees) are respected that they are honored and their offerings—the deadwood suitable for burning found on the ground—are used, unless a fire is for some other specific purpose. For example, among some in the Native American Church, where Chief Peyote is honored, a sacred fire is made only of oak on an earthen altar where a cross of sacred earth or sand has been laid. First, shavings are arranged in the shape of a V with the point toward the west, where the holy person sits. Then gradually the fire is built up until large timbers are burning, making a portal for the plant Chief Peyote to enter the circle and be with the people. Various angles are used in the building of sacred fires because spirit beings enter a circle only through a particular angle, as can be seen in pictographs and petroglyphs of the American Southwest that depict spirit beings entering a sacred circle, usually at about seventy degrees. For similar reasons, the mound builders of the American Midwest and Southeast oriented their earthworks within circles at angles aligned with various stars and star clusters, ranging from thirty degrees to seventy degrees, to allow the star beings to join in the ceremonies.

Sacred fires are generally constructed in the shape of a pyramid, tepee, or combination of both. To build a pyramid-shaped fire, choose two small pieces of wood and place them parallel east-west with tinder in the center, crossing them with two parallel north-south pieces, and then continue building the fire up to the desired height. For a tepee-shaped fire, place tinder in the center and arrange a circle of twigs placed upright, meeting at the top, to the desired size. Since the power of a sacred fire is in the flame, the fire itself need not be big, except when building a fire for a sweat lodge, which requires heat, or for a large gathering. In other instances, the sacred fire can be small and nurtured only with enough standing ones to keep it bright. Always, follow your inner guidance.

Establishing intent and selecting material for the fire should be done with conviction and integrity. To help establish intent when gathering standing ones, ask which ones wish to sacrifice themselves for the self-discovery or healing that is to take place. For example, look out across the landscape and ask aloud: "We are making a sacred fire today; who wishes to join in this ceremony for healing the earth and all beings?" The materials—actually, living beings—that volunteer by suddenly appearing more luminous or catching the eye with their clarity, however large or small, should be thanked, and an offering of cornmeal or tobacco given in return as a sign of respect and appreciation. Recognizing a contributing being's sacred mission builds an atmosphere of respect and gratitude to the ceremony.

Selecting the place for the fire also reinforces a ceremony's sacredness. The fire should be located centrally, where significant elements of the landscape come together, or where a certain feature of the landscape lends power. Just as the sun represents the

Creator's power to give life, so the sacred fire symbolizes the Creator's spark to provide guidance and healing. It becomes the Creator in the sacred ceremony, offering doorways for all beings to join.

Once the location is selected, make a sacred circle about fifty feet in diameter if it is for a large gathering, about ten feet in diameter for a small gathering, or as large as is comfortable if the ceremony is for you alone. Place burning sage or cedar in the center where the fire will be laid. Dig a pit a few inches deep to be used as an altar, carefully mounding the earth for it immediately west of the fire pit. Then place on this altar any sacred objects or items to be blessed. In addition, if you are carrying a *chanunpa*, or sacred pipe, a small pipe stand made of two Y-shaped sticks, with another stick laid across them in the Y, can be fashioned to hold the pipe, with its bowl touching the ground.

After digging the pit and placing sacred objects on the altar, gather all the standing ones and anything else you will require for your ceremony and place them in the circle, making sure that everything, including yourself, is smudged with sage or cedar smoke. Arrange the tinder and wood in the shape you have selected—pyramid, tepee, or a combination. Before lighting the tinder, invite all four directions (winds) to join as participants in the ceremony. Give each one a pinch of cornmeal or tobacco in gratitude for their presence; then give a pinch for the above (the Creator) and the below (the Earth Mother) and for all good spirits, ancestors, and power animals, thanking them for acting as gatekeepers to prevent any negativity or bad spirits from entering the circle. Finally, use a match or other flame to light the tinder, with a prayer of gratitude for the spirit of fire's participation in the ceremony. As the tinder ignites and as you lay small pieces of wood on the flame, listen to the flame speaking with the tinder and the wood, giving a message about whether the ceremony is a good thing. Pray or sing along with the fire and the standing ones, offering best wishes for them and all beings, inviting healing, health, wholeness, and positive light to shine in the world. If the fire, directions, and standing ones are all in agreement with your inner state and intent, the fire will grow quickly.

Every sacred fire has its own energy, which shows in its characteristics, such as how much smoke there is, the direction it blows from, and where it burns brightest. A smoky fire is female and will have the qualities of gentleness, compassion, and inwardness; a relatively smokeless fire is male and will be hot and burn quickly, offering much light for exposing truths and providing insights. A fire burning evenly in all directions will be harmonious. One burning quickest on the east side, however, will usher in new knowledge and perspectives, whereas one burning quickest on the south will promote healing, on the west will invite introspection, and on the north will offer truths that might be difficult to accept or deep insight and wisdom. A sacred fire will often provide a mixture of these energies, as the winds blow and flames change over time.

Once you have started the sacred fire, do not leave the circle without asking the fire's permission. Simply inquire, aloud or silently, "Permission to exit for a moment?" and wait for an answer. You will feel a response, which almost always is, "Permission granted."

If for any reason you receive a "no," look around and correct whatever might be amiss, then wait until permission is granted. Repeat this procedure when reentering the circle. Always, when leaving the fire, exit through the east, walking backward so that your back is never turned disrespectfully toward the fire. When entering, go in from the east and make one complete turn clockwise in place before stepping into the circle; turning clockwise honors the fire and the directions, and keeps the circle's energy flowing in the right way. If you make a mistake, do something thoughtless, or act badly for any reason while in the circle, simply ask for forgiveness from the fire, giving the negative energy to the fire, which will transmute it into positive energy. Or give a pinch of ground cedar wood to the fire and ask its forgiveness for any transgression that you or others have performed. Never throw trash in the fire or place anything in it without sacred intent.

When the ceremony is finished, allow the fire to expire naturally, without dousing it with water, and stay with it until it is completely extinguished. (Do, however, observe safety precautions: follow rules on public lands and, if for any reason you cannot stay with the fire until the embers have cooled beyond the point of reigniting, do use water to fully extinguish it.) After the ceremony is over, unless the circle is to be kept permanently, the earth from the mound should be returned to the pit and the land left as it was found. The circle can be deconstructed energetically by walking counterclockwise four times around the same path as before and thanking the Earth Mother and all beings for having allowed the ceremony to take place.

Just as a single candle glowing in total darkness seems to provide light far beyond its small size, so sacred fire extends beyond time and space into the universe. By recognizing and becoming one with its power, you will become more aware of the Creator's power within yourself.

A Simple Ceremony:
Us'ste'lisk (Sacred Fire Vision Quest)

In various tribes of North America, young people would often be sent on vision quests, or pipe fasts, spending days without food or water in order to receive visions and insights about themselves and the world, and commune with Spirit. Among the Cherokee, there is a way to do a vision quest using fire, called *us'ste'lisk*, in which the power for the visions or insights comes from the sacred fire. *Us'ste'lisk* can be done at any time by anyone seeking vision, insight, or healing.

The duration of *us'ste'lisk* is determined by however long it takes for the vision or insights to come and could last a few hours, a day, a few days, or a week. The procedure is essentially the same as that for doing ceremonies involving sacred fire, except you select thirteen river stones (grandfathers) to make the circle and you remain in the circle—other than leaving to get more wood if necessary—until the fast is over. If any negative thoughts, memories, or images come into consciousness, give them to the fire by holding a stick and mentally thrusting their energy through it and into the fire, or by reciting an affirmation such as "I give this to you, Creator! Thank you for your healing energy and insight!" Then feel what the fire (the Creator) gives you in return. Talk with the fire and listen for the message it relays back through its crackling and popping. Watch the flames to see what their shapes tell you, or what the coals indicate.

When the vision quest is over, you will know it. Allow the fire to die naturally. Finally, return the grandfathers to the wild, with your thanks.

From the Energy Notebook:
Holding Your Mouth Right

Sacred fires have their own being and personality. For example, once when I had been doing ceremony constantly over a period of days and was feeling rushed and frustrated, I prepared a sacred fire at a ceremony and despite the fact that all the wood was dry and should have burned well, I could not get it started. As I was wrestling with the fire, a tribal member drove up and wanted to watch. Heading over to her, I explained, "I'm having problems. Please just stand behind the tepee for a moment. I have to get myself right before I can get this right." She did, whereupon I sat by the stacked firewood to collect myself.

Suddenly I had a memory from childhood of an old man who used to take me fishing. One day we were in the boat in a backwater off a river and he was pulling a big, fat bream out of the water with just about every cast, while I couldn't catch anything, even when using his lures. Finally, he looked over at me, laughed, and said, "You're not holding your mouth right."

Stunned, I watched him and noticed that he was fishing effortlessly, almost lazily casting and allowing himself to be totally absorbed in the act itself, as if one with the river. I looked around, now deeply aware of the water gently rippling in the breeze, the sun shining bright, the birds singing, the blue sky, the boat gently rocking—all forming a moving picture-puzzle of natural beauty. While absorbed, I felt a tug on the line and pulled up a fat bream. Not caring if I caught a fish, just enjoying the day, I noticed my creel slowly beginning to fill.

After experiencing this memory, I looked at the firewood carefully piled to provide the Creator's power for this ceremony, and laughed, realizing that the spirit of fire was only waiting for me to get out of the way! "Thank you, Creator, for this beautiful day and the opportunity to do this ceremony for people," I whispered, with gratitude. With that, I touched a match and the sacred fire flared up high, as if its energy had been pent up. The ceremony went flawlessly, progressing in its own way and time, as was meant to be.

Water

Although some people think that stones or earth are the oldest substance on the planet, before there were any land forms water covered the earth. All the wisdom traditions and many cultures have myths and legends about how land was formed from water, and indeed, every living thing is composed primarily of water and can be seen as an energetic lattice holding water. All the water that has ever existed upon the earth is here now— in rivers, streams, lakes, oceans, clouds, air, and all living beings—and it is up to us, as caretakers of the earth, to ensure that it is clean, respected, and honored, as opposed to polluted and despoiled.

Moreover, human beings are directors of water. It has been proven that thoughts and emotions such as anger, jealousy, love, compassion, and forgiveness actually determine the crystalline structure of frozen water, or ice.[1] The ability of the body to direct energies that change the chemical makeup of water has been well documented, particularly in studies of kinesiology. Indigenous peoples around the world have known this for millennia. In ancient times, for example, when people prayed over their food, they didn't just clasp their hands together and give thanks, they actually used their hands—the chakras, or energy centers, of the palms—to change the vibrational rate of the food, also composed largely of water, by allowing the Creator's healing power to alter its chemical composition. Those who could channel the most healing power through their hands to bless food were recognized as holy people—for they had the ability to purify food for the body, mind, and soul. In the days before pasteurization, homogenization, and artificial preservatives, such prayers over food were considered a matter of life and death, not merely a perfunctory gesture of thanks.

Indeed, before putting anything in the mouth—food or water—it should first be blessed in the following way. Hold your hands over the food or water and say a prayer, such as this: "Thank you, Creator, thank you, Earth Mother, for providing this sustenance. May it lead to nourishment of our bodies and its energy go out for the healing, health, and wholeness of all our relations. *Aho.*" The underlying belief is twofold: that germs and viruses cannot survive in food and water with a high vibrational rate and that such food and water is more easily converted into energy the body needs.

Not only can blessing food or water purify it by changing its composition, it can also transmute food or water into other substances, for example—water into wine. In the Bible, Jesus told his disciples that they could do as he did and he wished to teach them so they could teach others; indeed, Peter walked on water until he began to doubt and sank (Matthew 14: 25–33). One of my teachers, a Lakota medicine man, told of growing up on the reservation when there was no food. His father, a medicine man as well, created food out of energy, which they all ate and not only survived but grew fat. Many spiritual masters, such as yogis and holy teachers, have manifested food from energy. And in fact, anyone with the intent can do it, by gaining control of all energetic systems of the body, having faith in the transmutation, being at peace with oneself, and remembering to ask if the transmuted energy will allow itself to be used in the manner intended.

In other words, if we follow Spirit, we can change food or water from one substance to another simply through intent and allowing it to happen. If, for example, you already have fully developed palm chakras, say through Reiki attunement or healing hands work, you can have a lemon on one side of you and a glass of purified water on the other, go within, and allow the essence of the lemon to pass through you to the water. This is done in the following way: put the lemon on a kitchen counter to the left of you and a glass of water to the right; hold your left palm down and open a few inches above the lemon and your right hand the same over the glass of water; feel, or receive, the energy of the lemon with your left hand; transmit that energy through your right hand;

then taste the water. Our energetic vibrations have such an effect on substance that longtime alcoholics frequently have the vibration of alcohol so embedded in their energetic systems that merely holding a glass of water, even long after recovery from alcohol abuse, can cause that water to taste of alcohol.

Similarly, essential oils derived from aromatic and medicinal plants can have an effect without being ingested. One simply holds them in the hand and allows their vibration to heal where healing is needed.

In ceremony, water prayed over becomes holy water, which can be a powerful medium for purification and healing; indeed, it is used for such purposes in virtually every religious tradition. Positive outcomes result because when we heal something, we are primarily transmuting water as it expresses itself through the energetic pattern of the person or thing being treated. And ceremony, which raises the vibrational rate of all in attendance, since people are comprised mostly of water, is actually an efficient way to help everyone within the sacred circle and beyond. When we do ceremony to cleanse water, we are doing ceremony for the whole world, which is connected through water; the spirit of water pervades everything.

Simple Ceremony:
Healing Bowl/Dreaming Bowl

When doing ceremony, whether with large groups or privately, such as *us'ste'lisk*, the power of prayer to change water should be kept in mind. A simple ceremony for gaining knowledge for healing self and others is called Healing Bowl/Dreaming Bowl. Take a bowl—either an average food bowl or one specially chosen or made for this ceremony—fill it with tap water, and put it on the altar or in the circle or medicine wheel where the ceremony is to take place. The power of the ceremony itself will bless the water, making it holy water. This water can then be used in other ceremonies: a naming ceremony for an infant; a ceremony for purifying and blessing people by dipping sweetgrass in it and sprinkling the water on participants or passing the wet end of the sweetgrass across their brows or third eye chakras; or a healing ceremony to remove negativity from the body of an afflicted person.

This container of water can also be used as a dreaming or divination bowl. In antiquity, when Cherokee women were in their moon time, they would often keep such a bowl of water by their beds and, awakening during the night, gaze into it to obtain prophetic visions. But it can be used in a similar way by anyone immediately upon waking in the morning, to induce visions or insight. After using the bowl of water for divination in this way, it is beneficial to write down such impressions for further thought.

From the Energy Notebook: "Going to Water"

Among the Cherokee, it is believed that water once was the only living substance from which all other life derived, and that it therefore has many powers. In the past, every day upon rising, Cherokee people would follow the practice of "going to water," completely immersing themselves seven times in a nearby stream or other water source—rain or shine, summer or winter, even breaking ice to get to the water. This practice astonished early white settlers, who didn't take baths often. Most Native Americans considered Europeans filthy, especially since, living in nature, their own olfactory senses were highly attuned.

This practice of "going to water" was, however, not just for hygienic purposes but also a spiritual act, done to purify body, mind, and soul. A modern-day Cherokee once asked me if she was behaving nontraditionally by not "going to water" like her ancestors did, since there were no streams around her home. "Do you shower?" I asked. "Of course," she said. Then, I told her, it does not matter if the water flows down a stream or through metal pipes, as long as the act of "going to water" is done in a sacred manner, with gratitude to the Creator, thus purifying body, mind, and soul. It is more pleasing to the senses and inspiring to the spirit if we are surrounded by rocks, hills, sky, and clouds when we "go to water," but we must accept what is given to us. Although energetically, immersion in water is in itself a healthy act in that both the physical body and spirit body are cleansed, when done with joy we are honoring the water itself wherever it may be. By treating water in a sacred manner, we allow it not only to cleanse us but also to heal the Earth as it cycles from land to sky to land, among all beings.

Earth

Among the Powers, none is more powerful than the Earth Mother. Often called "Gaia," she is a living being, encompassing all elements—fire, water, earth, and air. All things on Earth spring from the Earth Mother. Her heart is fire, like that of the Creator, so hot that her molten core is liquid rock. Her blood is water, running in streams, rivers, and oceans; and her tears are rain, making growth possible and washing everything clean.

Her body is earth, a living substance that gives life. She breathes as we do, with winds that circle the globe, inhaling and exhaling through plants and trees that purify and enrich her breath. She gives us everything: fire and shelter from cold, as well as shade and cool breezes to alleviate heat; food in the form of plant and animal people that sacrifice themselves so we might live; water for us to drink; materials from which to create clothes, build houses, and even entertain ourselves in creative ways.

Because all things on this Earth spring from the Earth Mother, in concert with the Creator, we begin every ceremony by expressing gratitude to her in order to open the heart for miracles to happen. Then throughout the ceremony, we keep in mind various energies of the Earth to enhance the potential for self-discovery or healing. When thinking of Earth energy, we naturally think of gravity, but the power of Earth goes far beyond that. One aspect of Earth energy may be thought of as two spirals, one winding outward, the other inward. The outward-winding spiral energy reflected in such things as the germination of a seed with its upward, outward motion of potential. The other spiral can be seen in such things as the withering and dying of a plant, which the Earthly Mother draws back into her.

A second aspect of Earth's power is violence or chaos, as reflected in volcanic activity. A third aspect of Earth's power is magnetism and gravity, demonstrated each time the Earth draws things to it.

When doing ceremony, several techniques can be employed to optimize the expression of Earth power. One technique is to use symbols in connection with

Earth energy, such as the cross and the crescent. These are two of the best-known symbols because of their associations with Christianity and Islam, but they were also known earlier to Native American cultures. The cross represented the choice of different lifeways—one often called the Red Road, representing unity, and the other the Black and White Road, representing division.[2] The crescent symbolized both potential and manifested energy, or that which has yet to be revealed and that which has been revealed. In ceremony, if a cross is used, the energy will be direct, perhaps even confrontational, and will show dualities; if a crescent is employed, some unexpected results may occur and other hidden aspects may be revealed later, reinforcing the eternal truth that not everything can be known.

An especially effective use of these symbols can be seen in a sandpainting. Sandpaintings can be simple, displaying only outlined symbols, or elaborate, with designs of many colors. They may be made of sand, various soils, or clays of different colors that have been gathered in a sacred manner. But always they are created in harmony with the Earth then given away to the Creator and the Earth Mother with blessings and no regret. Following the ceremony, even those that were exquisitely made with painstaking effort requiring many hours of craftsmanship are allowed to fade or be scattered so they become one with the Earth. Releasing them without attachment imbues the ceremony with that much more power.

To make a sandpainting, first collect sand, soil, or clay in a sacred manner, gathering it, for example, from a creek bank where the water flows fresh and clear, giving cornmeal or tobacco in return; for city dwellers, purchasing sand, such as from a pet shop, is fine, but before using it, run water through it with the intent of clearing all energies, allowing it to dry in the sun for its blessing before using. Then, where the ceremony is to be performed, clear the earth of vegetation in the shape of a circle—perhaps within your fire ceremony area. With a twig or quill of a feather, draw a symbol and dig out the earth from the center of the symbol, removing about a quarter inch of dirt if the symbol is a foot long, or an inch if the symbol is three or four feet long. Finally, fill the symbol with the sacred sand and do ceremony, the outcome and the flow of which will be affected by the Earth's energy.

A second way to harness Earth energy is through creating a permanent public space for doing ceremony. Most indigenous peoples have such spaces, usually an arbor or a stone circle such as a medicine wheel. An arbor is a sacred circle usually fifty feet or more in diameter, bounded by wooden rails in the center of which is a permanent fire pit and altar. The fire pit itself may contain a smaller circle bounded by wood or stones that is entered only by the elders, the firekeeper, or those with offerings for the sacred fire.

Stone circles, seen in various forms around the world, were most likely used by medicine people or priests for sacred ceremony. Some have lines of stones radiating out to the directions and to features of earth and the sky, such as the rising sun or moon, or constellations— providing connections to star beings and star nations for celestial orientation. Others are more elaborate, with "gates" and stones set inside to represent certain energies or spirits for various purposes, such as sacrifice.

As with the location of the other stone circles around the world, the location of a permanent public medicine wheel in which people can find solace or do ceremony or meditation should be chosen with care. Walk across your land and look for a spot where the land forms seem to converge or where various elements of nature, such as hills or water, seem to be in perfect proportion. When you find such a power spot, you will feel it in your heart; your mind will clear; your hands may tingle; the birds' calling might seem more vibrant, the colors around you more intense. (In ancient times, stone circles were often built along the earth's energy lines, or ley lines, where the power of landscape features was the most potent.) This is where you should place the center stone or fire pit and build the altar after it is consecrated by a medicine person or holy person to create the sacred space and ensure it has power.[3]

The medicine wheel could be fifty to one hundred feet in diameter and have four "gates," or openings of two stones at each of the cardinal directions to allow the powers of the directions to enter, as well as for people to come in for their walking meditations. Because people will enter the medicine wheel from the eastern gate, it should have a special stone near the entrance, perhaps just outside it to the left, that will perform two functions: to be a place where sage and water can be put so people can cleanse themselves before entering the circle and to act as a "gatekeeper" to keep bad spirits out and invite good ones into the circle.

Further, since it is a public circle, it would enhance the circle's energy and unifying aspect if people were invited to bring stones to add to it, which is how native peoples of the past built monuments, each family or band bringing baskets of local soil or stones. If the number of stones grows to exceed the space available for the ring, you can do as ancient peoples did and start a new ring perhaps one hundred feet away that would mark an event, such as where the sun rises at summer or winter solstice, or spring or fall equinox, as seen from the vantage of the central stone, or the rising of a star cluster, such as Orion or the Pleiades, which many tribes, including the Lakota and Cherokee, honor as ancestors.

Around the central stone, you may wish to put another, smaller circle for a meditation area, perhaps filling this new circle with crushed rocks if a central fire pit is not planned. If the medicine wheel is to double as both a meditation area and a place for ceremony, the fire pit can be located in the central circle of crushed rock and left open when not in use, and low stone benches could encircle the fire for people to use while meditating.

The protocol for use of the medicine wheel is as follows: Before entering, individuals must pause at the eastern gate to purify themselves with sacred sage smoke and by dipping the hands into clean water and brushing off the body. After entering, they go from right to left, toward the south, around the circle clockwise, pausing at each gate to acknowledge and give thanks to the power of that direction or "wind" and feeling acknowledgment from it in return. Individuals can then move around as guided or pay homage to the central stone—the Creator's stone—or area for the sacred fire, and meditate there or participate in ceremony. Once the initial cleansing, entering, and acknowledging have been done, people may exit through any gate. To do so, they must walk clockwise (or sunwise) right to left, facing the central stone and walking out backwards so as not to turn their backs toward the central stone.

At ceremonies, a fire may be made in a pit on the eastern side of the central stone, representing the Creator's fire. In such instances, someone should be the designated firekeeper, to light and tend the fire in a sacred manner night and day until the ceremony is complete, at which time the fire is allowed to die on its own. The sacred ashes may be taken by participants to use at home in ceremony or carry in a medicine bag.

To use such a medicine wheel as a labyrinth to gain insight into situations and answers to perplexing questions, first write down a question and put it in your pocket. Next, enter the circle in a sacred manner and walk once around, honoring each of the directions and thanking them for insight and answers. Then continue to walk slowly around the circle, pausing when Spirit directs, and allow insights to arise. At some point, you will feel that an answer has been given. Leave then in a sacred manner, giving thanks to the directions. Even though it may be several hours or days before the answer emerges fully into consciousness, an attitude of humility and respect ensures that insights eventually will come.

Simple Ceremony:
Using Earth's Power to Ground,
Center, and Cleanse

We can draw healing energy from the Earth at any time, since, the power that propels life on this planet is constant. Some people go to great lengths to ground and center themselves—doing all kinds of rituals, such as going barefoot or taking a long pilgrimage to another place. But you can do this anywhere, inside or out, and adapt it accordingly. The Earth's energy, as reflected by gravity, is strong and reaches all locations, even through glass and steel. The Earth's energy is strong. We need only open our body, heart, and mind to her to fulfill our potential—a procedure that can be assisted by the following ceremony.

Lie or sit cross-legged on the earth, or stand with the base of your spine against a tree, feeling how your body is one with the Earth. Feel the Earth energy coming up through your buttocks or feet as you breathe in; as you breathe out, feel it in the middle part of your body, between your abdomen and heart. Feel power in the area just below the navel, the *hara*, and let it radiate out all around you. Now you are grounded, centered, one with the Earth energy.

Breathe in and feel the Creator's light, divine energy, come down from above through the top of your head (crown chakra); breathe out and feel the Earth energy centered between the abdomen and the heart. Now you are one with the divine energy from above and the Earth energy, meeting in your *hara.* You are in the place energetically where you can do ceremony, healing, directing of energy, near or far, with the help of guides and angels, merely by allowing your attention to go wherever it is needed. In this state, you are what you were meant to be, a child of earth and sky.

Cleansing often enhances one's ability to use the Earth's power for healing. If you need cleansing, such as after a traumatic event or in preparation for doing ceremony, the best way to do this is to bathe yourself in sage smoke, brushing it from head to toe. If you do not have sage, you can cleanse yourself in the following way: Rub your hands together then grab your left hand with your right and pull the energy out, throwing it to the ground, where it will be neutralized by the Earth; then grab the other hand and do the same. Next, blow on your hands with the thought of the most sacred light you can imagine, the energy of the north, the ancestors, wisdom, and highest beings; then with your hands brush yourself from head to toe and finally pat the ground.

To cleanse even more thoroughly, use mudras—that is, make a circle with the thumb and first finger of each hand, breathe in the Earth's energy, hold the air in your lungs for 30 seconds or so, then release, making a circle with the thumb and second finger of each hand and keeping your lungs empty for 30 seconds. Next, fill your lungs, still doing the second mudra, hold for 30 seconds, and release, switching to the third finger and thumb. Repeat with the fourth finger and thumb. As you inhale each time, bring in Earth energy from below; as you exhale, bring in sky energy from above, expelling all negativity and toxins, allowing Earth and sky to cleanse you. Finally, imagine yourself in a three-dimensional bubble of light.

From the Energy Notebook: Use Symbols With Care

We do monthly ceremony here using drums with the medicine wheel, and occasionally I'll incorporate a symbol in the medicine wheel, as guided.[7] As outlined, I'll gather earth and fill the symbol with sand that has been gathered along a creek bank in sacred manner, forming it in an earthen plate that is placed in the medicine wheel. Usually, the symbol is the crescent; allowing knowledge to unfold during and after the ceremony. But one time, I don't know why, I was guided to use a five-pointed star. The ceremony itself was very electric; the air seemed to crackle; people's emotions were all over the map during the ceremony, some laughing, some weeping. In the days after the ceremony, momentous changes occurred in everyone's life who had attended: one woman became pregnant, another broke up with her husband, two people fell in love finding their life partner; as for us, a few days later, a drunk driver slammed into our cars parked in front of the house – which wasn't altogether bad, as no one was hurt and we had been pondering selling these two old cars to buy one better car and the insurance settlement solved that issue. The point is: use of this symbol in this way, in an already powerful ceremony, accelerated the energies and accelerated change. Symbols are powerful. Be careful in the ones you choose and know that using them will have consequences.

Air

Even before there was water and earth, there was air, or the quality that would become air. In wisdom traditions, air is associated with spirit, the life force, and the breath. In Eastern cultures, it is called *ki, qi, chi,* or *jing,* the power that animates and unifies. In Hinduism, it is called *prana*, the life principle, that which distinguishes animate from inanimate, the vital breath that is equated with the *atman*, or cosmic essence. The Greek word *psyche* is believed to have originally meant breath and came to denote spirit. The ancient Egyptian god Amon was also equated with breath, the mysterious source of life. In Hawaiian it is called *ti* or *ki*; in Polynesia, *mana;* and in Lakota, *niyan,* meaning air, life force, the breath of the wind that we share with all living things.

The power of air can be harnessed for use in ceremony because it aids in the transmission of words and thought forms. We think of air as being empty space because it's invisible and our bodies move through it easily, but it's not; nor is it simply a dense compound of oxygen that can be measured. Instead, it is both a crystalline medium along invisible threads that connects all things and transmits energy, as well as a matrix that surrounds the globe. It is at once discrete, held by all beings within them, and connecting as one indivisible force. When the ancients said they heard something in the wind that told them what someone said or what might occur in the future, it might not have been sheer imagination they referred to, but a reflection of air's power to transmit electromagnetic forces. The voice is more than sound waves moving through air; it is an electromagnetic force that broadcasts thought waves through the medium of sound. If you and a friend are walking two hundred yards apart and you shout at him, he may not hear the words because of the density of air and other sounds, but on a different level he might hear the impulse of the thought.

That is why when doing ceremony we should be careful what we utter. Not only does air give spoken words a new life, but the force of ceremony provides power of its own. Thus, words spoken ritually have a power that transcends all normal usage. It is said among medicine people that spoken words are heard two ways: in the manner in which they are heard by the person to whom they are directed and the way they are heard by Spirit, which entails the intent behind them. If, for example, you tell your child, "Don't touch the stove, you might get burned!" your child hears the literal meaning of the words and hopefully will not touch the stove. But what Spirit hears is the love or anger behind the words, the implicit meaning. It is such intent behind the words that gives prayer its power.

The medium of air also carries both positive and negative thought forms—the patterns of energy generated by thoughts—and thus certain settings can be either uplifting or damaging. An example of a positive thought form would be a prayer that our ceremonies go out into the universe, and each person leaves the ceremony acting on that impulse, performing kind acts so that the love expressed becomes manifest in the world. Each person carries that energy with them, so that not only are their behaviors positive, but their attitudes are healing—causing smiles, relief, diverting others' thoughts from fear and anger or troubles afflicting them. An example of a negative thought form occurs when one driver accidentally cuts off another, who then shakes his or her fist and mutters threats. This creates a pattern of energy that can actually "blast" the offender and even lodge in the person's aura, or energy body, until eventually entering the physical body, resulting in dis-ease. Shamans throughout history have learned to extract such intrusions of negative energy so that illness won't occur or, if already present, will disappear. Among energy medicine disciplines, such as Reiki, removing these lodged thought forms is called psychic surgery.

The fact that the air transmits electromagnetic forces and carries thought forms means specific locations on Earth, as well as the Earth itself, can be affected by the positive or negative energies transmitted. Some areas have positive energy and are thus good locations for sanctuary or for obtaining insights, such as certain formations of hills and valleys or relationships between water and land. By contrast, some sites tend to be infused with negative energy patterns, for example, such as places where lightning strikes often or where volcanic eruptions occur. People, like nature, can also produce negative thought forms in a location where there would naturally be positive ones, by placing asphalt over land, bulldozing or clear-cutting trees, disrupting the land, or otherwise creating imbalances on the earth. Such imbalances can cause tremendous disruption in the form of earthquakes, tsunamis, and hurricanes, as the Earth tries to rebalance herself. Ceremonies can be conducted to heal particular imbalances—for example, where asphalt has covered free-flowing land forms, clearing ceremonies might involve giant medicine wheels hundreds of miles in diameter where people hold ceremonies simultaneously.[4]

Perhaps the most impressive use of the power of air is when a holy person holds a chanunpa, or sacred pipe, and makes prayers, breathing the smoke into the air to carry each prayer around the Earth, thus connecting the prayer-giver with all beings, seen and unseen. We can all learn to send prayers around the globe by setting good intent and praying out loud from the heart. Like the well-known example of the butterfly effect, where the beating of the wings of a butterfly in Africa can cause a hurricane in America, our prayers in the medium of air can gain power if they emerge from the heart, drawing energy voluntarily gifted by all beings—rocks, insects, water, dogs, horses, spirit beings—to spiral around the Earth. Even simple ceremonies can aid in this process.[5]

Simple Ceremony:
Prayer Flags

A simple ceremony using the power of air for healing the self and others involves the planting of prayer flags. These don't have to be elaborate. To make one, take a piece of cloth and, while saying a prayer for healing, rip off a strip, tie it into knots, and fasten it to a tree or to a stick that you then place in the ground. Your prayer will be picked up by the wind and carried where it needs to go to effect healing.

Simple Ceremony:
Earth Healing

To do an earth healing ceremony, create a sacred circle perhaps ten feet in diameter, and in the center place five stones. Ask the directions, or winds, to join you; ask the goddesses of earth and sky to join you; ask your angels and power animals to come; and thank all these spiritual beings for the miracles they are performing to bring balance to the Earth. Then either drum, sing, or meditate, connecting with the Christ Consciousness Grid (the plume of Quetzalcoatl), the encircling layer of energy above the earth where the highest forms are held. Set your intent on bringing balance and harmony to the earth and all beings, allowing the energy of the earth to peacefully relocate along crystalline lines of air. Within this matrix allow the sky paths to the holy ones to open so that the way is made clear to become one with earth and sky. Thank the four harmonies for correcting any mistakes or omissions, or for adding any necessary prayer, thought, or act. To end the ceremony, say "amen," or "*aho,*" or "*mitakuye oyasin.*"

The Sweat Lodge *(Asi/Inipi)*

The idea behind the sweat lodge, called *inipi* (purification lodge) in Lakota and *asi* (literally, hot house) in Cherokee, has existed in different forms in many parts of the world, including the artesian baths of the ancient Greeks and the sauna of Nordic peoples. Native Americans used three basic types of sweat baths and their variations: the hot rock method, in which water is poured on the stones (grandfathers), used by the Navajo and Sioux (Inipi), as well as all tribes in the central plains, the Southwest, and the eastern woodlands; the direct fire chamber, heated by blazing logs, used by the Cherokee; and a heating duct system believed to be of Mayan origin, practiced by tribes as far north as the Aleutians.

Use of the sweat lodge as practiced by the Lakota has become a pan-Indian activity adopted by the descendants of various Native American tribes, and has even become part of popular culture. Among some traditional peoples, such adoption of Native American sacred ways by non-native people is a source of controversy and resentment.[6] So, if you choose to build a sweat lodge, be forewarned that you may encounter such attitudes. As with other ceremonies, the most important aspect of any sweat lodge ceremony is intent, which should be to provide healing to self and others and to generally add positive energy to the world by expressing gratitude to the Creator, compassion, and a desire for healing and wholeness.

When constructing a sweat lodge, everything should be done in a sacred manner, taking care to keep thoughts and words positive. To build a small sweat lodge, first create a sacred circle in the chosen location, as described in chapter 3. Each of the four directions should be marked by a flag or strip of cloth on a pole in the proper color: east, red; south, yellow; west, black; north, white. Next, gather sixteen willow saplings each about one inch in diameter and up to twenty feet long, in a sacred manner by asking permission, seeing which ones volunteer, and leaving behind a token of gratitude, such as tobacco.

Then proceed to build the lodge by placing twelve saplings in the ground in a circle about eight feet in diameter, after digging a small hole for the base of each and putting a pinch of tobacco in each hole, with a prayer to the Creator, the Earth Mother, and all beings that the lodge meet their approval. Bend the saplings to meet and tie them together using cloth or twine to form an inverted bowl. Make the entrance facing east by bending a sapling and sticking both ends in the ground to form a rounded door, the eastern gate. Construct the western gate in the same way opposite from it. Then bend two saplings around the lodge to hold the other saplings in place. Further, place a special "lightning stick," which can be a staff or sacred cedar pole slightly bent from the western gate to the eastern gate, over the top to represent the connection to the star nations and spirit beings.

Next, in the center of this frame dig a hole for the grandfathers (stones) about two feet in diameter and eight inches deep. Using the removed earth, create an altar by mounding it about five feet from the entrance. Then make a path, or "sacred way," about twelve feet long from the lodge to the east. There, leaving a four-foot gap, dig a hole for the fire pit where the sacred fire will be built to heat the grandfathers.

To ensure total darkness in the lodge, cover it with a layer of blankets and then tarps, which may be plastic but preferably canvas, since it breathes. Finally, make a door, which may be a special blanket. Between times when the lodge is used the frame is left up, while the coverings can be left up or taken down as desired.

Simple Ceremony:
Opening to the Powers of the Sweat Lodge

All the powers—fire, water, earth, and air—are incorporated into the sweat lodge. As such, it becomes a medicine wheel of the earth, within the womb of the Earth Mother. The sacred fire is the Creator's fire, the fire of life. The spirit of water circulates constantly, through breathing and sweating. The point of reverence for the Earth is the altar; the road each being must walk on the Earth is the sacred path. And everything is connected through the power of air, through which the directions, the winds, come in to carry the prayers out into the world.

To build the fire for the sweat lodge, while keeping in mind the principle for making sacred fire, choose two large pieces of wood and set them parallel east-west; fill the space between them with tinder; cross them north-south with the grandfathers laying on the north-south layer to cover the east-west pieces of wood entirely. Once the grandfathers are piled on, make a tepee of large logs completely surrounding the inner pieces of wood and the grandfathers. When preparing for ceremony, logs should be constantly added to the tepee as they burn, until the grandfathers are ready for the lodge.

As for the grandfathers, they should be selected carefully. River rocks will work, but lava rocks are best. Avoid rocks with quartz in them, however, as they will explode from the heat, and do not use sandstone or granite, which tend to crumble. When spotting potential grandfathers, approach them in a sacred manner, asking if they wish to sacrifice themselves for this purpose. Only take those that volunteer, and leave a gift, such as tobacco, in their places.

A typical sweat lodge might have eighteen to thirty-six grandfathers. But be apprised, the number of grandfathers really doesn't matter; a lodge with forty grandfathers could feel "cool," while one with eight could feel intense. Some people are fond of saying, "I went on an eagle sweat with seventy-two stones!" implying that they are strong because the lodge was so hot. A sweat is not meant as an endurance test, however, but rather an opportunity for prayer, receiving visions, and sharing wisdom. We perceive the wisdom of the grandfathers as heat, but it's actually energy. The lodge can seem "hot" with only one stone, whose wisdom, unlocked by the Creator's fire, greatly increases the energy of the lodge. Regardless of the number of grandfathers, it is their wisdom, transmitted by the spirit of water passing through our bodies via breathing and sweating, that allows us to circumvent the rational mind and become one with the Creator, thus giving us power and insights, and effecting healing. The people in the lodge receive visions, guidance, and healing because they are sacrificing themselves, along with the grandfathers and standing ones (the wood), for all beings, their prayers going out to the "hoop of life," where everything benefits through giving and receiving.

A typical ceremony consists of four rounds. The protocol involves asking the grandfathers themselves at the start how many and which of the grandfathers should be used. If a ceremony is to have, for instance, twenty-four grandfathers, five might be used for the first round, five for the second, and seven for the third and fourth, although some lodges use only even numbers of stones. Generally, five are laid down first, representing the four directions and the center (above, below, the Creator), then the others added. As each grandfather is brought in and put into the lodge's fire pit, it is blessed with sage or other sacred herbs or touched with sweet grass, and thanks is given. Once the grandfathers are in place, the door is closed and the water pourer (the lodge leader) sets five dippers on the grandfathers, one for each direction, signifying the start of the sweat. The lodge leader may then ask those present to pray or sing a sacred song. The song need not be a recognized sweat lodge song but could be as simple as "Twinkle, Twinkle, Little Star" as long as it's sung from the heart and offered with prayer, in a good way. This first round could be dedicated to healing the self (since one's basket must be full in order to give to others). The second round could focus on family (both blood relatives and those adopted into the participants' sacred circles). The third round, often called "the women's round," could be dedicated to women, with women singing songs and giving prayers, or to healing. The fourth round might focus on the Earth and all beings.

The duration of a round is determined by the inclinations of the lodge leader and participants and is generally over when everyone becomes silent. Then a prayer of thanks is given to the grandfathers, along with four dippers of water, and the door flap is opened. Fresh air comes in, and the people may cool off and lie down and rest before the next round. Generally, it is not advised that people leave the lodge until the four rounds are completed, but someone who has to leave must do so between rounds. A person can usually come back in the lodge after the first or second round, but generally must stay for the duration if they come back after the second round. This is because the rounds build upon themselves, increasing in intensity and power until, by the end, everyone emerges transformed in a positive way.

Despite the great physical and spiritual benefits of the sweat lodge ceremony, it can be taxing. Therefore, people with medical conditions such as hypertension (high blood pressure) and heart problems should forgo direct participation or check with their physicians before participating. Also, the water pourer, or lodge leader, should be adept at helping people with ailments, and preferably have first-aid training, including knowledge of cardio-pulmonary resuscitation. And caution should be taken to avoid getting burns from the fire or the hot stones or overexertion from hauling wood or handling the heavy stones. People with medical conditions can still come within the sacred circle and sit next to the fire, in any direction that is a sacred spot for them, and many lodges have benches set up for this purpose. Naturally, all who are within the sacred circle, whether part of the sweat in the lodge itself or sitting outside the lodge next to the fire, are participating in the ceremony and should comport themselves in a sacred manner.

Further, although women who are in their moon time (menstruation) are not allowed within the sacred circle, their presence near the circle can add significantly to the ceremonies. Often a moon lodge is erected outside but adjacent for such women to participate in the ceremony, helping to increase its power. Women in their moon time are not excluded from the lodge because of notions about being "unclean" or because of discrimination but because they are considered to have such great power during their moon time it could disrupt the sweat lodge or any other sacred ceremony. Although their presence in an adjacent moon lodge is most welcome, it is up to each individual woman to decide to attend or whether isolation is preferable. (See section entitled "Moon Lodge.")

Some common rules for the sweat lodge are the following:

Sacred area: The circle outlined by the flags of the four directions is a sacred circle. When ceremonies are under way, the people outside the lodge as well as those within the circle should be in prayer or silent meditation, with no unnecessary activity or noise. The area between the altar and fire is holy and should be respected. The firekeeper oversees any activity within the sacred circle once ceremonies are under way. Nothing is to be placed in the sacred fire except by the firekeeper, who, along with a designated helper, must tend the fire. Littering is forbidden. Drugs or alcohol are never allowed; participants are expected to be sober and respectful of others at all times. Women in the moon time are not allowed within the sacred circle or lodge, since their power at that time is so great.

Altar: The lodge leader puts the sacred pipe on the altar on the north side; gifts to the lodge leader are placed on the south side of the altar; the west side is kept open for foot traffic; the east side is open for items to be blessed by the ceremony. Pipes may be placed on the altar, bowls toward the west, with the lodge leader's farthest north. Staffs may be planted east of the lodge leader's. Stepping over the sacred altar or sacred fire path is not allowed; crossing is permitted between the altar and the lodge or on the east side of the sacred fire. Only the firekeeper may step between the lodge and the sacred fire.

Dress: Participants in the lodge ceremony should dress modestly. For women, this usually means a simple cotton dress to the mid-calf or ankle; for men, shorts, and shirts are not required. Towels are permitted inside the lodge, but other items require permission of the lodge leader. No metal should be worn in the lodge.

Entering the lodge: Before entering, take a pinch of tobacco from the can next to the altar and offer it to each of the four directions, starting at the east and proceeding clockwise, and sprinkling a little on the altar. Then gift tobacco to the sacred fire before presenting yourself at the entrance to the lodge to be smudged with sage by the doorkeeper. After being smudged, kneel at the door and thank the Earth Mother, asking the lodge leader if you may enter. The lodge is entered on one's knees before moving clockwise as far as necessary to reach an available seat.

Preparation: Most individuals who participate in a ceremony are there for an intense spiritual experience, so they may fast or pray for a day or two in advance, although this is not required. A light meal several hours before the ceremony is OK, but heavy meals are not advised. Since the ceremony can last for hours and involves sweating, it is a good idea to drink plenty of liquids the day of the ceremony, though not immediately beforehand.

Ceremony: The lodge leader chooses the type of ceremony and how it is conducted. Silence is to be maintained unless the lodge leader says otherwise. If moved to speak, ask, "Permission to speak, lodge leader?" Often the lodge leader will call on individuals to speak, or ask if they would share their thoughts, or if they would like to sing a sacred song. When finished speaking or singing, signify by saying, "Aho," "Amen," or "*Mitakuye oyasin.*" Only the lodge leader and the firekeeper handle the grandfathers.

The ceremony lasts as long as Spirit directs. There are four rounds, each usually becoming hotter with more grandfathers added each round. Between rounds, the door is opened for fresh cool air to enter. It is acceptable to leave after one round or two if the heat is too intense, or for health or other reasons. If it is necessary to leave the lodge, wait until the end of a round then ask the lodge leader for permission to leave. After leaving, the lodge leader's permission is required before reentering. Only the doorkeeper may touch the door at any time. People who do not wish to enter the lodge can pray outside the lodge on the south side of the altar, where they are still participants within the sacred circle.

It is not unusual for spirits to enter the lodge during the ceremony, and in fact, they are specifically invited. Odd or unusual colors, shooting lights, and sounds are often heard, since the intense heat provides new doorways to perception. The best way to tolerate the heat is not to think but to feel and pray—out loud if it helps—and to remember to breathe. The ceremony is a sacrifice for healing and visions, and the intent is never to harm but to help everyone in the sacred circle and all beings of the Earth Mother.

Gifts: Since most items used in ceremony, including tobacco, white sage, and up to a third of a cord of wood, cost money, giving the lodge leader a gift or donation is appropriate and much appreciated, although there is no charge for the ceremony and no gift is expected. Generally, participants are expected to bring food and drinks for feasting after the ceremony, some wood for the fire (if possible), and a stone if they have one they believe would add good spirits.

Moon Lodge

Menstruating women are often prohibited from participating in sacred ceremonies because at such times their exceptional power due to their connection with the Earth Mother, the forces of nature, and Spirit is so great it overshadows the power of sacred ceremonies in proximity. Consequently, when sacred ceremony is done among Native Americans today, there is frequently a tent or enclosure just outside, where everything can be seen and heard, for women who are in their moon time. They are honored and the people are grateful for their power, which can add immeasurably to the ceremonies through their participation in this way.

Moon time is a sacred period when women become one with the Earth Mother and the Creator, capable of discovering invaluable inner knowledge, and able to access the power of prophecy for the benefit of all. For this reason, many Native American peoples do not recommend the customary vision quests or pipe fasts for women. Instead, for thousands of years among various indigenous peoples across the world women have had moon lodge.

Among Native American societies of the past, because women lived in close proximity, through the principle of resonance their cycles would usually coincide. When this time came, often with the full moon, the women, including those too young and too old to menstruate, would go to the moon lodge, where the older women would attend to the women in their moon time, and the young girls would learn the traditions and lore of the tribe from the older women. This practice united women and helped them maintain their heritage.[8]

A young girl's first menstruation was a sacred event that blessed all the people. It was marked by much ceremony, with special clothing prepared for her and people coming from all around to give her gifts and receive words of wisdom and prophecy from her. During this time, she was instructed by the medicine women, considered the wisdom keepers of the tribe, about how to comport herself from that day forward, her rights as a woman, and trials she could expect in the years to come.

Additionally, sacred, secret rituals regarding the use of menstrual blood, many having to do with the blessing of crops, have been handed down in various tribes. These and other ancient ways of honoring the moon time transition and its sacred blessing are worth resurrecting.

Simple Ceremony:
Creating a Moon Lodge

A simple way to honor the sacred menstrual time is to construct a tent, tepee, or pavilion in nature to serve as a moon lodge. Such a lodge should be built and occupied only by women so that it is devoid of male elements. It should be within a sacred circle created by women and energetically purified by women by smudging and making offerings of tobacco or cornmeal before use.

Women may wish to meet at a set time each month when one of them is in her moon time, using the event to do sacred ceremony for themselves, sharing their knowledge, perhaps with added input by women beyond the age of moon time. Experience at the lodge should be divided between time set aside for solitude and quiet reflection and time for activities focused on helping and supporting one another, such as discussing mutual concerns, reading poetry, drumming beneath the moon, singing songs, or sharing special food and teas that provide strength. The demands of daily life should be set aside, even if only for a brief interval, for rejuvenation and seeking insight and wisdom.

One ancient ceremony that can still be done today is for a woman in her moon time to go out into the fields beneath the moon and simply let her blood flow, becoming one with the life-giving Earth Mother, allowing the light of Grandmother Moon to purify and rejuvenate her. If there is no place in nature to celebrate the connection with the power of earth and sky, simply honor the body, quietly acknowledging its powers and those of Spirit during this time.

From the Energy Notebook: Honor the Urgings of Spirit

It was not originally my intent to include information about how to build and use a sweat lodge, as this very sacred activity can be easily abused. I've been in lodges where people don't know what they are doing, including lodges run by Native Americans, some of which were even sexually exploitative. Understandably, many spiritual elders frown on sharing sweat lodge knowledge, and that was also my view before the following experience occurred.

For years here, people had been asking if I ran a sweat lodge and I had always said, no, that I didn't feel qualified. I had attended lodges for years, but it's quite a different animal to be responsible for one and lead one. Then, a man who ran a lodge out West for several years moved here and beseeched me to open a lodge. Every time he saw me, he would say, "PathFinder, this is something you have to do, for all the people whose lives you touch." Then, while I was visiting friends in Arkansas, a Cherokee elder whom I admire completely out of the blue urged me to start a lodge to help the people who come to me. Doc, a man who had run sweats with the California prison system for more than a decade, even offered to come to my house in Mississippi to help me build one. I told all these people I would think and pray about it and get back to them.

Shortly thereafter, I went on a spirit quest, a twelve-hundred-mile circular medicine wheel trip from Mississippi through Arkansas, Oklahoma, Texas, and Louisiana, then back to Mississippi. While near the Medicine Mounds where Comanche chief Quanah Parker spent his last days in Texas, I was drawn to a store that seemed to sell Native American items. Out of the blue, again, the store owner, a Paiute, asked, "Do you have a sweat lodge?" I laughed, and told him that part of my quest was to resolve that very question. Then he told me how he had come to run one. Two sets of friends with whom he sweated were at odds, and each decided to create their own. "This is wrong," he told them, the lodge was meant to resolve differences not sustain them.

"Fine," they said, "you try running one!"

"But I don't feel qualified to run one," he answered.

"You can learn," they said, and at their insistence, and so as not to break up the friendship, he built a lodge and ran it for them all to enjoy.

"How long have you run your lodge?" I asked.

"Sixteen years," he answered. We both laughed.

Spirit had given me my answer. Upon my return to Mississippi, Doc showed me how to build a lodge in a sacred manner.

Later, a friend, Michael Touchstone, told me he was going to build a lodge, and when I asked him how he had decided to do so, he answered Spirit had told him to. I asked if an elder was going to help him. He said no, he was just going to build it the way he believed was right.

This caused me some misgivings, since I believed from my training that a lodge had to be built and initiated in the right way. Although I don't believe I ever told Michael not to build the lodge, I did tell him it had to be done the right way, and I'm sure he felt my disapproval.

A few months later, Michael and his partner Cyndi were visiting and Michael seemed to have a bad cold he couldn't shake. We did a sweat, which should have cleared his head but didn't. My perception was that his illness went deeper, that there was something he just couldn't let go of regarding his Vietnam War experience many years before that was causing him pain. I told him that if he wanted to come to do a special sweat, it would take some time and effort, but he might be healed. Because he lived several hours away, he declined.

A few weeks later he was diagnosed with cancer, and despite my offers to come sweat, he was too weak to make the trip. He died three months after the diagnosis.

I couldn't help but wonder what might have happened if I had actively encouraged him to build his own sweat lodge as a healing place. This experience made me realize that no one should be discouraged from pursuing the guidance, vision, or help for healing they intuitively seek, or be told it must take place in a certain way. Consequently, information about building and using a sweat lodge is included in this book to underscore the importance of honoring the urges of Spirit and as encouragement for individuals who feel they may need to do so for personal healing. Thank you, Michael, for teaching me.

Power Objects, Quests, and Rituals

When doing ceremony in nature, it's almost certain that power objects, items carrying great energy, will manifest in some form. Such objects, given by the Creator, spirit beings, or the Earth Mother, are meant as gifts to be used in ceremony and, while being transported, should be kept in a sacred manner, preferably in a medicine bundle or medicine bag. Similarly, ceremonial quests and rituals require certain protocols to keep them sacred.

Medicine Bundle and Medicine Bag

A medicine bundle contains objects you wish to keep sacred and separated from other objects, which have their own medicine. For a while, I carried a medicine bundle that included the ritual objects for firekeepers among the Cherokee until they could be passed to a suitable candidate to be trained as a firekeeper. Also, as a ceremonial elder for a group it was my duty to carry its *chanunpa*, or sacred pipe, as well as a prayer stick, which were kept in separate bundles because each had its own medicine. A medicine bundle is considered alive and thus treated with respect and honor.

If you have obtained something of power that needs to be kept separate, you can make a medicine bundle. First, find suitable cloth—the vibrational energy of red is thought to have protective qualities. Next, enclose the object in it along with some sacred sage or other herbs, and secure it with cloth ties, then keep it in a safe place for future use.

When transferring a medicine bundle to someone, it must be done in a sacred way, either before a sacred fire, passing it over the fire four times, or in a sacred spot. First, thank the powers for protection of the medicine bundle. Next explain out loud the significance of the bundle—how it operates in a good way, how it was obtained, and the purpose for which it is being conveyed with best wishes. Then offer it ritually four times to the person, who should accept it after the fourth offer.

A medicine bag contains all the things that may be required for particular ceremonies. For example, I am frequently asked to pour water while visiting people who have a sweat lodge, so I have a medicine bag that includes a water dipper, "medicine" for the grandfathers, sage, matches, and a prayer fan, as well as certain power objects that have been gifted for possible use. It also holds the *chanunpa* in its own bundle, and various paints, or medicines, used in sacred dance. In addition, I have two other medicine bags. One, kept in the trunk of the car, holds various items for ceremony, including cloth for prayer ties, bags of tobacco for ceremonial use or for gifts to medicine people, a healing bowl, sweetgrass braids for ceremonial use, sage, and other items suitable for gatherings. The other medicine bag, which can be carried, contains crystals, stones, feathers, and other items used for healing ceremonies, as well as various power objects gifted by Spirit. Items from each of the three bags can be mixed and matched, depending on what's required. Unless you are doing ceremony for large numbers of people, or are frequently asked to do ceremonies of all kinds on the road, one medicine bag should suffice.

A medicine bag can be made of any material; some are fashioned of ornate, beaded leather, fur, or fancy cloth, but a simple tote or duffle bag suffices. Such a medicine bag is sacred, should never be touched by anyone other than the owner without permission, and has a function different from the small medicine bags worn around a person's neck, often hidden under clothing, which usually hold special items—crystals, stones, tobacco, feathers, fetishes, snakes' teeth, or other objects—that reflect personal power. The personal medicine bag may be worn all the time, especially if a person is on a vision quest, but is usually kept in a larger medicine bag, or in another sacred place.

Portable Spirit House

Among the Cree, Ojibway, and Algonquin tribes of North America, people of spirit would often carry their sacred house, or spirit house, with them, in the form of a special skin or skins sewn together, for the purpose of communing with Spirit. This would assure them that *Kitchi-Manitou*, the Great Mystery, Creator, was with them always and would appear to them in many manifestations.

For example, an individual seeking wisdom could be walking and perceive *Manitou* (Spirit)—perhaps through hearing a sound that might be a spirit ally, seeing a bird that looked a certain way, or sensing disharmony among the elements of nature. The person could then unwrap the sacred bundle; make a sacred circle, walking around four times and chanting; then sit down and drape the skin over a small bush or prop it up with a stick, or just wrap it around himself or herself to create a small, dark tent. Once inside this spirit house, the person would perhaps light a tiny fire, or burn herbs, asking that the space be made sacred.

The person would then silently sing a sacred song arising from the heart, or one the family or clan had handed down for calling in *Manitou*, and await any vision or knowledge from Spirit. Then the wisdom from Manitou's heart song would merge with the person's heart song until the wisdom sought was found. In this way, a person can connect with Spirit at any time, and glean understanding, or be informed of events, or the thoughts of loved ones, far away. This portable sacred house has power and can be constructed by anyone.

Simple Ceremony:
Making and Using a Portable Spirit House

Today, a portable spirit house can be made of a special blanket used for this purpose, kept in a clean and holy knapsack, travel bag, or other special medicine bundle in the trunk of a car when traveling. Remove and use it when Spirit might be heard. For example, when driving to a remote area or walking in the woods and suddenly feeling stirred by a birdcall or a voice in the wind, cover yourself with the blanket, draping it across a bush or propping it with a stick gifted by the standing ones to form a tent. Inside, create a sacred circle, making an offering to the four directions, perhaps burning leaf or sage or sprinkling some tobacco on the Earth Mother, then listen for any messages from Spirit, being sure afterwards to express gratitude.

The Sacred Pipe, or Chanunpa

When hearing about the pipe of Native American peoples, often broadly referred to as the "peace pipe," people generally think of the Plains Indian pipes and stories of the sacred pipe of the Lakotas (the *chanunpa wakan* of the OcetiShakowin, the Seven Nations of the Sioux) as told by Black Elk.[9] Among the Lakota, Dakota, and Nakota Oyate, the *chanunpa* (pronounced CHA-new-pah) refers to the buffalo leg bone pipe given by PtesanWi, or White Buffalo Woman, and other similar carved pipes of catlinite, or pipestone, mined in Pipestone, Minnesota. It is considered *lela waken,* very sacred, as is the white buffalo, which is connected to prophecies about the birth of a white buffalo calf as a sign of the reappearance of White Buffalo Woman to reinstate balance and spiritual harmony among all beings. Consequently, among the Sioux Oyate, for anyone to carry a *chanunpa* without being called to do so and having the blessing of a Sioux holy person is considered sacrilegious.

Pipes are not exclusively of Sioux tradition, however. The practice of smoking the pipe as a means of connecting with the Creator is thousands of years old and was practiced by most native peoples of the Americas, as archaeological evidence shows. The early chronicles of the Spanish in the Southeast, and the French and English in the Northeast, tell of native people beginning meetings with smoking the pipe, or calumet, and each tribe has its own story of how the sacred pipe came to them. Among the Cherokee, for example, the sacred pipe was given by Uktena, "The Keen-Eyed," a great serpent so powerful that simply to gaze upon it resulted in instant death. Pipes were made of a variety of materials, including clay, catlinite, or argillite, the red mudstone found at Pipestone, Minnesota, and carved or molded into various forms, including animals, spiritual beings, deities, and phallic fertility symbols. The type of tobacco that grew wild in the Southeast, *Nicotiana rustica,* was traded throughout the continent for smoking in various pipes. So, apart from the modern hostility among some people who claim the sacred pipe belongs to one group over another, the traditions of the sacred pipe is varied, long and deep.

The sacred pipe in all its forms has power that should not be underestimated. Once, for example, a Sioux holy man visiting in Mississippi was severely injured during an attempted robbery and called me to come do a pipe ceremony with him at the hospital. For safety reasons, the hospital personnel said the only place we could do the ceremony was outside in the nurses' smoking area. Although it was a barren area with only tufts of brown grass, as he said his prayers the grass turned green and began to grow. Another time, I was invited to do an Earth healing ceremony in Natchez, Mississippi. The next day, to honor my host, I invited her to do pipe ceremony. She said she wished her boyfriend, who lived in New Mexico, could participate, so I told her to call him on the cell phone and he could participate long distance. Afterward, he told her that his entire neighborhood had been transformed during the ceremony—everything grew quiet, many dogs came and sat respectfully at the edge of his yard, birds flew in as well, and his house was filled with beautiful light for days.

The power of the sacred pipe, which cannot be explained by logic, is the physical expression of the power of the Creator. It is holy because people keep it holy, and its power transcends that of any single human being. Further, the power of the sacred pipe is derived from its marriage of male and female energies as a reflection of creation itself. The bowl of the pipe is the female energy; the stem is the male energy; when the bowl and stem are connected, the pipe is creation itself. All that is said and thought when the pipe is held in the hands becomes a thought in the mind of the Creator. The smoke is the prayer that goes out in the medium of air, connecting all with the divine, making the prayer one with the Creator.

Being a pipe carrier, either male or female, is a calling, and can be done only by a person who is open enough to allow the power of the pipe to work through him or her and who has knowledge of the sacred ways it is to be used. In addition, those who carry a pipe are often humble and honorable enough not to advertise their abilities and knowledge. For example, at a recent gathering where a new pipe was being activated, all who carried pipes were invited to smoke the new pipe and offer their own pipe so that all the pipes' energies could mix and empower each one. Out of a group of about twenty people, seven individuals produced pipes, none of whom had previously given any indication they carried pipes. By contrast, I've seen people who had a pipe but were not suitable to carry one, with the result that the pipe soon disappeared in some way, was lost, stolen, broken, or given away.

Further, the manner in which a pipe is obtained is essential to its utility and power. Perhaps the best way to get a pipe is to be gifted one by a spiritual elder. It is also possible to buy a pipe. And although purchasing a pipe is frowned on, one can be respectfully purchased if done in the right way—by first feeling called to carry one then having it cleansed, blessed, and activated by a holy person. Another good way to obtain a pipe is to make one, first carrying the materials for a while to see what the Creator suggests as a shape, then after fashioning it, having a holy person or medicine person bless it.

The pipe I use most now was made by a series of special individuals and the vision of how it should be came to me in a recurring dream. Since I'm not dexterous at carving, I eventually called a Cherokee woman who carves pipes, and serendipitously her husband, an Ojibway, had had a similar dream and said he would make it for me. He, in turn, told a Sisseton-Wahpeton Sioux friend, who saw it in dreamtime, too, and made it, although it needed a stem. I described the stem to yet another Cherokee woman who lived in Texas and she recalled one like it made by a Sioux in Iowa and drove to Iowa and got it as a gift from the man. Then a woman of Iroquois ancestry gathered walnuts in Massachusetts and sent them to be used in staining the stem while yet another woman, of Sauk and Ottowan ancestry, made the pipe bag. This pipe, indeed, is the product of The Great Mystery, is it not? Now, whenever this pipe is smoked, all these people's thoughts and energies add to the blessings of the ceremony and receive blessings in return.

The late Fools Crow, one of the most revered Sioux holy men of the modern era, often had pipes made to his specification after he dreamed about them, then he gave them to select individuals, something I routinely do as well.[10] There is no doubt that the energies involved in obtaining, making, or gifting pipes contribute to the power of any ceremony and the general ability of the pipe to effect positive energy and healing. In the Cherokee way, pipes were fashioned from many different materials, often of clay, and could represent any deity, or dream, or wish or desire. All pipes made in sacred manner have power and should be honored, from whatever native tradition they derive. For several years, I carried a wooden pipe that had been fashioned in Singapore; finally giving it as a gift to a special Lakota woman who cherished it.

Simple Ceremony:
Smoking the Pipe

To perform the ceremony of smoking the pipe, reverently take your pipe from its bundle. Lay the bowl and the stem, which are always wrapped separately, on the wrapping—for example, red cloth. Burn sage over the pipe and breathe the sage smoke through first the stem then the bowl, thoroughly smudging them. Next put the stem in the bowl, holding the bowl against the Earth Mother and, if necessary, wetting the stem with your lips and tongue before inserting it into the bowl, for a tight fit. Then breathe the sage smoke through the bowl and stem together, ensuring they are both clear.

Load the pipe with the bowl upon the earth, offering a pinch of tobacco toward each direction, starting with the east, as well as a pinch for the Creator above and the Earth Mother below, and all good spirits before filling the pipe—usually with 100 percent tobacco without preservatives, although this can be mixed with various herbs. Pick up the pipe, always keeping the bowl near your heart, with the bowl in your left hand and the stem in your right, and hold the pipe up to the sky as an offering to the Creator. Move the stem clockwise toward your mouth and light the pipe. Once lit, offer it again to the Creator stem first, letting the Creator take the first puff. Then move the stem clockwise to your mouth, take deep breaths and motion for the smoke to cover your head and body; breathe out the smoke as a prayer; say your prayers holding the pipe and, if with others, pass the pipe to your left, always with the stem moving clockwise, the pipe held in both hands, left hand on the bowl, right hand on the stem. If the pipe goes out while traveling around the circle, tamp down the tobacco and relight it as before.

After the ceremony, once the pipe has burned out, the ash should be either saved for a later ceremony or given to the sacred fire if one is burning. The pipe should then be immediately disassembled and reverently repacked; or, if in a lodge sacred circle, placed on a pipe stand or on the altar until the ceremony is concluded.

The pipe should never be openly displayed except in sacred ceremony and should always be honored. Spirit says the pipe is to be taken out only when it is the proper time, and never on demand. In any situation, ask the pipe if it should be brought out, and heed its wishes. Sometimes, it will ask that it be loaded and not smoked, just carried. This usually means that it has a specific place and purpose in mind for which you are to carry it. Spirit, through the pipe, will always guide you as to where to go and what needs to be done.

The ceremony of smoking the pipe can be done alone in nature, with all the spirit beings, power animals, and spirits of the lands and water, or alone in the home, or in groups where the people form a circle, sitting on the ground. It is a powerful ceremony. In the hands of a holy person or medicine person, it can perform miracles, but in the hands of someone who does not honor it, great harm can result. The thoughts and prayers of those participating in the ceremony can provide insight, guidance, and effect cures of those present and at a distance.

Simple Ceremony:
Prayer Stick Training

For people who do not have a *chanunpa* or have no intention of following the way of the pipe, a prayer stick is an alternative avenue to guidance and healing that can be used anywhere by anyone. I learned this when, years ago, I obtained my first *chanunpa* and was terrified of it. Although it came to me at the right time and place, and I knew what it was used for and how it was used, I didn't feel ready for the responsibility of holding such an instrument of creation in my hands; I feared its power and didn't trust myself to speak truly. I admitted my fears to a trusted elder, who laughed and said, "Try a prayer stick, using it longer and longer each day, until you feel confident enough to smoke your pipe."

So I fashioned a prayer stick out of a piece of cane cut from a creek bank around which I wove my wampum, made in the original way that the Peacemaker showed, choosing beads to represent sorrow, joys, events, and things for which I was grateful in my life and weaving them together, the beaded work acting like a prayer for healing.

Thereafter, each day I took the prayer stick from my medicine bag and practiced holding it and speaking my truth. It took a great deal of practice to learn how to speak truly from my heart, without deception, rather than from my mind; to stay present and not be distracted by events of the day; and to speak affirmations, with forgiveness for self and others. Over time I learned to speak from the sacred space within, and found healing, solace and power.

After accomplishing this with a prayer stick, I picked up the pipe and smoked it, speaking my truth, with my words turning to prayer. The key, I discovered, is that when holding the prayer stick, you can speak only inner truth from your heart, which often requires considerable introspection, intuition, and prayer. What you say may not make a great deal of sense, since it's based on emotion, not logic, and you may repeat yourself because truth may emerge piecemeal and over time, but your truth will eventually come out, and all the resentments, hurts, and dishonesty will be replaced by healing, compassion, peace, and joy.

A prayer stick may be fashioned of any material; some are elaborate, beaded, each bead attached with a prayer; others are simple, a branch from the ground with cloth tied on it. Whether intricate or simple, the object should be fashioned, treated, and held as sacred. When holding it, only speak from the heart, not the mind. This may mean many hours of silence, but the exercise will teach discipline, the pathways of truth, and the ability to discern the sacred space within and be able to utter it.

From the Energy Notebook: The Pipe Carries You

When Annette Waya and I were returning in August 2006, from the Peace Village, a very special place in Vermont operated by Sun-Ray, an international spiritual society dedicated to planetary peace, we were reminded of the power of the Sacred Pipe.

The Peace Village is overseen by Dhyani Ywahoo, chief of the Green Mountain Ani Yunwiwa (Cherokee people) there and the 27th generation holder of the Ywahoo ("Great Mystery") lineage of spiritual elders, and just as she is the epitome of the old time, traditional "peace chiefs," a spiritual elder and leader of great depth and knowledge, the place is of very high vibration. So, we were flying quite high, so to speak, when we left and were preparing to board our flight at the Manchester, N.H., airport.

During the security screening, though, I was singled out, and shunted aside because there was something "suspicious" in my carry-on baggage: The Sacred Pipe.

At the security table, as soon as I saw what was the object of their interest, I told the inspector that it was a chanunpa, a holy object, and I would prefer that only I handle it.

You would have thought that I had said "Hello, my name is Osama bin Laden and, if you will excuse me for a moment, I'd like to light my shoe."

Suddenly, I was surrounded by big, burley Transportation Security Administration officials with badges and uniforms. The supervisor—a large, rather intimidating fellow—was summoned. I will never forget it.

Now, normally, I'm a rather unassuming type, would rather pass undetected anywhere, without causing a fuss, certainly not opposing armed "authority" and the subject of law enforcement. I'm six feet tall, but the supervisor was easily half a head taller than me and twice as broad, and with his face six inches from mine and eyes boring into mine, I repeated my request: "This is sacred, holy, and I would prefer that only I handle it."

However great the risk, or fear, this was something I had to do.

The pipe is serious business. The pipe was around before any one of us was born and it will be around after any mortal now living has passed. It is more important than anyone who carries it; but whoever carries it must carry it in the right way, even if it means peril. For, without respect, and sacrifice, then what is its meaning? The pipe carrier must live up to the pipe; for if he or she does not carry the pipe in the right way, then the pipe carrier is not honoring the pipe, all who carry and have carried the pipe, or shown the proper respect for those who will carry the pipe, honoring it and its traditions through the generations. If it meant my next stop was at the U.S. prison camp in Guantanamo Bay, Cuba, or a hospital recuperating from being forcibly "detained," so be it. The pipe and its traditions will endure, even if the flesh is weak.

After a seeming eternity, the supervisor, apparently having sized me up, said, "OK, if that's the way it is, take off your jacket, empty all your pockets, pull them out, and keep your hands in plain view."

Relieved, a little anyway, I did as he ordered, and proceeded to unwrap the pipe from its bundle, explaining some of the symbols on the outside (my power animals, spiritual connections), unwrapping the red cloth (sacred color, for protection), noting and letting them sniff the white sage scattered about it (there for purification), the tobacco (just "normal" tobacco), some of it gifted from other spiritual elders—we share these things—a few herbs (all legal), and finally taking the stem from its wrapping and the bowl from its bundle (explaining they are always kept separate until actual ceremony takes place), and holding them for all in the circle of security guards to see.

Once the pipe was revealed, the energy of the moment suddenly shifted. The face of the once-menacing supervisor suddenly changed from one of sharp inspection to utter delight, like a child at Christmas when a gift long under the tree is finally opened. "Oh," he said with a lilting voice, with the expression of a young boy: "A peace pipe!"

"Well," I said, "some call it that."

And I proceeded on to explain about the pipe and what it means.

The TSA guards blended back into their work, all except one: a woman. She had a few more questions about the pipe, and ceremonies associated with it, as I wrapped it back up, each piece in respectful manner. I told her that I was writing a book that would soon be coming out (this one!) and, perhaps, she should read it, if she wanted to learn more.

Then, she said something that shook me to my core.

"How long did it take you to learn all this?" she asked.

I had to honestly think. "Hmmm. Seven years," I answered.

"You must have had very good teachers," she replied.

It occurred to me then that this was the real reason why I was shunted aside. Not for "security." Not for "terrorism" or any fear-based thing, but for Spirit, to give the gift of light, and love, in a place that sorely needed it. Yes, I thought, and what is the lesson here?

I was holding the feather I use to clean the pipe (metal is never to touch the pipe) and I asked her if she would mind if I did something. "Certainly," she said. I took the feather and began brushing her lightly, her face, her forehead, her hair, arms, torso, gently brushing away all negativity. "This is called a feather blessing," I told her. It's easy to do and can be done at any time, by any feather, perhaps a robin feather, or wren feather, whatever is found, and if she would go out a few times per day and gently brush the feather from her head to her feet, she will remove all negativity, all tension and fear. In her job, I told her, surrounded by fearful, nervous people, it would be a good thing to do—grounding herself with the Earthly Mother, feeling the wind gently caress her as she does this thing, perhaps listening to the birds speaking to her. She would return refreshed, and invigorated, full of light, protected, and one with all.

When I finished, she thanked me, and Annette and I went on our way.

The lesson is this: For those who carry the pipe, remember: The pipe carries you. You never know where it will take you, or what will be required. It may require courage, and conviction, but always love. If, in carrying the pipe, you follow the way of the pipe, all will be well.

The Vision Quest, Fast, or Pipe Fast

The vision quest, fast, or pipe fast has become popular in recent years because it's a direct way to experience nature in all its power, learn to commune with spirit beings, find direction, and generally gain insight into the meaning of life. For various indigenous peoples, a vision quest is often done by young men (or sometimes young women) as they approach adulthood for the purpose of gaining insight into the ways of nature, Spirit, and their place in life on Earth. Medicine people or holy people do vision quests differently, however, and for a variety of purposes, including to honor someone who has passed away, to celebrate a great event, or to provide guidance and wisdom when someone is troubled. The important thing is that while in fast, everything is holy and has power; it is a doorway beyond ordinary reality.

A vision quest is often called a pipe fast because usually a person must first perform a vision quest before he or she is considered ready to carry the pipe. The fast teaches how to see, hear, and understand the Creator's powers and differentiate thoughts (ego/personality) from what is really real—all skills necessary for using the pipe and speaking truth from the heart. It does not mean it is the person's calling to carry the pipe, only that the person is prepared if called upon by the Creator to do so.

Although a four-day vision quest has become the most popular form of this ritual, there are many other ways to achieve the same goals, such as *us'ste'lisk*—being alone with fire, as practiced by the Cherokee—putting the seeker in a covered pit for days, or taking the person up a mountain for a succession of days. And while fasting is a central theme of such vision quests, a "fast" can technically amount to refraining from any substance or activity to show mastery over one's body and sacrifice. Abstaining from food or water in a desolate spot for four days is a form attributed to the Lakota but is more pan-Indian. For example, Peter V. Catches, a thirty-eighth-generation Lakota medicine man of the Spotted Eagle Clan, has been leading pipe fasts for many years in the tradition of his clan.[11] He will take a person for a first fast for one day, a second fast the same time of year the second year for two days, then three days the next year, and finally four days the next. This traditional Lakota practice demonstrates an individual's commitment and allows the person to absorb the lessons learned during the fast time in ways that last.

People often come to me wanting to be "put out," or sent on a vision quest. Months beforehand I explain the various ways it is done and the person describes what he or she expects from the fast. Generally, the first morning, at dawn, we will sweat, then the person will be put in a sacred circle. The next morning, at dawn, I'll check on the person and see if what is sought has been found or if another day is required. This procedure will continue for however long it takes the person to receive what was sought. Then we will sweat, and the person will describe the visions in the lodge to attain greater understanding and so that they become real in the world.

Without this type of sharing, it can be difficult for the seeker to comprehend the visions or even acknowledge them. For example, a woman who had been "put out" complained to me that she had spent the entire time waiting for a vision and all she had seen was an ant when she had expected something dramatic like lights, images, kachinas, or the hand of God reaching down. What she failed to understand was that the ant was God. Had she gone more deeply into the experience and seen the true power of everything that occurred, she would have realized the vision of the ant was a great gift, embodying an important insight about the inter-connectedness, the oneness of all things in creation. But her attachment to ordinary reality had prevented her from appreciating the true magic of her fast.

When going on a fast, it is important that an elder, or trusted person, "hold center" for the person on the fast—through also holding vigil at a distance, holding the person in prayer, checking on the person and so forth. This provides the grounding needed so that the person on the fast can have a point of reference to maintain some attachment to the material world, as well as provide perspective once the fast is over.

In addition to the guidance from a holy person in interpreting visions, elders often make the vision quest last four days because, they say, it takes that long for a person to hear what the Creator is saying and to absorb the most important lessons of the vision. Regardless of which variant of the vision quest a spiritual elder advises, it is potentially a powerful ceremony for self-discovery and healing.

Simple Ceremony: Painting the Sky

In modern society, it's difficult to be totally present and immersed in the beauty of nature, one with the elements. Some of the ceremonies that have been handed down through the centuries may seem intimidating to individuals today, with their time schedules and need for creature comforts. Fasting, time spent without a specific focus, and the idea of becoming one with nature can seem daunting. Sandpainting, however, can be a less stressful avenue for connecting with nature and preparing for a more prolonged and demanding vision quest.

An insightful type of sandpainting to create, called "painting the sky," involves using colored sands to match every color of the sky within a twenty-four-hour period, spiraling toward the center of a circle as time progresses, so that at the end of twenty-four hours the center will be the color of the outermost band. First, assemble sands of many colors, either through gathering them in nature or purchasing them at a hobby store. Next, find a spot in nature where the sky is visible and you will be undisturbed for twenty-four hours. If you live in a city, consider camping out in a suburban friend's backyard. Beginning well before dawn, create a sacred circle and clear a circle within it of rocks and pebbles. Start with the color of the dark sky, using black sand or mixing blue-black sand and pouring it along the outside perimeter of the earth circle. As time progresses, mix sands to match the color of the sky and proceed around the circle. This activity will give you a purpose while you seek insights and guidance.

If twenty-four hours seems too daunting, try painting the sky from daylight to dark, then spending the night in prayer or Dreamtime, allowing yourself to integrate the lessons of nature.

The Spirit Quest

A spirit quest can be considered a pilgrimage without a specific destination, similar to the ceremony Australian Aboriginals call a walkabout. The purpose of a spirit quest is to follow the dictates of your spirit to learn lessons about how Spirit is in everything and about your soul's purpose in the journey we call life.

Because we spend so much of our lives in unconsciousness and routine, we have become unaware of the miracles of Spirit constantly around us and must step out of our everyday lives to find what is within. The destination of a spirit quest is therefore unimportant, but the quest requires that you be totally present, so old habits and ideas don't dictate your perceptions, making you unconscious, and thus leading you away from Spirit. In addition to breaking old patterns of thinking and behavior, you will also want to leave behind emotional baggage that has you continually attending to your inner dialogue, judging yourself and others, and creating limitations and barriers to your perceptions. The reason for being totally present in a spirit quest is to see the *wakan* (sacred) in every object and event, thereby learning from Spirit so your strides toward growth and healing become longer, your life more fulfilling.

Ultimately, a spirit quest is not a journey to some great mystical "beyond"; indeed, the reality of each moment is greater than any projection of the mind. Instead, it is an inner journey to build a greater appreciation for reality and your place in it. Although it is not necessary to leave your home or neighborhood to go on a spirit quest, being away from your customary surroundings is likely to aid in the search for Spirit. Because people often become lulled by surroundings they are used to, forcing yourself away from your comfort zone of the usual can help you see life with new eyes. And if finding the mind of the Creator and opening our eyes to miracles requires going to new places with expectations acting as goals for action, then such a spirit quest has meaning because upon returning to your surroundings you may realize the path of Spirit within you. In addition, it is helpful to go to sacred sites where the "walls" between ordinary and nonordinary reality are thinner and perceptions of the truth more expansive.

At the same time, it is a delusion to think you will find greater truth outside of yourself in some external environment, even if it is a sacred site. If we are truly on the path of Spirit, we seek to create conditions so that we can glimpse the mind of the Creator in all we do every day, wherever we may be. If we were truly perceptive, we would find the world in a dew drop, the universe in a song—and a spirit quest is a reminder of that truth.

Simple Ceremony:
Going on a Spirit Quest

To go on a spirit quest, first devise a general time frame and itinerary to help create perspective. For example, say, "I want to be in such and such place on such and such date." I usually time my spirit quests with workshops or conferences. So if I'm due in Crestone, Colorado, on April 7, I'll head in the general direction on April 1, knowing I have to be back on April 14. Also, some time before April 7, I'll hold my hand over areas of a regional map to see which ones "call" to me. Although many people make a spirit quest into a journey shaped like a circle or figure eight, the specific form is not as important as following Spirit's guidance. During the quest, whenever faced with a choice about which way to go, I'll always "check in" and see what Spirit advises.

Be aware, however, that Spirit has no sense of time as we know it. Once, Spirit kept telling me there was a place I needed to be up ahead. I kept checking in, asking Spirit if I would be there soon, if I had farther to go, and so forth. For about two hours I kept getting "yes" for an answer. Finally, after eleven hours of apparently rambling this way and that, I checked in and Spirit told me the place was near. I drove another 100 yards and saw a sign for the road Bear Mountain, pointing right. "Here?" I asked. "Yes," came the reply. I drove up the mountain and arrived at a desolate spot seemingly at the top of the world just as the sun was setting and the moon was rising. Finding it to be a magical spot, I did vigil there that night. The experience made me more aware of the vast difference between our conception of time in the everyday world and the spirit world, and also made me remember that what counts is not the destination but the experiences along the way.

Distance Healing

There are times when power objects must be used to heal people at a distance. Such occasions are called for especially when those who need healing are unable to attend ceremonies. It should always be remembered that when one is in the sacred circle one creates, one is connected to everything and time and space mean nothing. Whether a person to be healed is physically present or far away makes no difference; we are all related, all connected in the tree of life when doing ceremony in sacred space.

Simple Ceremony:
Healing at a Distance Using Crystals

Healing a person at a distance can be accomplished by using a crystal and a tripod. First, make a tripod by wrapping three sticks together at the top with string. Next, tie on a crystal so that it hangs down at the center of the tripod. Then fashion a doll or other item to represent the person needing healing, or write the person's name on a piece of paper and place it under the tripod. Program the crystal by holding it in your left hand and feeling the energy from your heart flowing into it. Then leave the tripod and crystal up to effect time-release healing, reprogramming the crystal occasionally. Such healing action can go on for days or weeks, if needed.

If for any reason a tripod is unwieldy, healing at a distance using crystals can also be done in the following alternative way. On the ground or on a piece of paper, draw the ancient healing symbol Umane (OO-ma-nay), a square with four short lines extending from each corner. The Umane symbol is square because it represents only a part of the earth—specifically, that which we can see or know. The lines going out symbolize the earth power beyond that portion, extending out into the universe. This symbol is frequently in pictographs or petroglyphs in the American Southwest and is universal though the name used is Lakota.

Within the Umane, draw a circle that represents the sun. Place the doll or piece of paper containing the person's name in the circle and program four crystals with heart energy, placing a crystal at each corner of the Umane so that the crystal's tip is within the circle. The Umane represents the Earth Mother's healing energy; and the circle symbolizes the sun, the Creator's power as expressed through light and air. The crystals with tips placed within the circle, act as bridges between earth and sky for healing. You can also use the Umane and sun symbols with a tripod. Further, since the energy of the Umane is that of the Earth Mother, you can increase the power of the ceremony by making the Umane of earth in the following way: dig a small square with corners stretching out like triangles, about one inch into the earth, or beneath the level of vegetation. Make a circle with sun-bleached sand, or earth that has been dried in the sun.

Prayer Sticks

Prayer sticks are used in ceremony to offer prayers to the earth and sky. There are two basic types: those designed for repeated use that may be intricately carved, beaded, and sometimes have bones, feathers, or crystals attached to them; and those meant to be destroyed after ceremony. Permanent prayer sticks should be made in a sacred manner—carved respectfully, all the while calling in the powers to help, and each bead woven with a prayer. If bones, feathers, or other items are attached, they should have special spiritual significance that will help guide prayers to the Creator.

By contrast, temporary prayer sticks can be simple, just a stick of wood that is carved, covered, or tied with fabric or yarn, but still made in a prayerful way. The colors of the cloth used may denote the directions of the medicine wheel and their powers, or they may have special significance only to you. By giving energy in prayer while fashioning prayer sticks, you are receiving energy, too.

Following ceremonial use, it is best to leave temporary prayer sticks behind, gifting them to the Earth Mother, the ribbons then acting as prayer flags to transmit the prayers. But they can also be burned in a sacred fire, in this way gifted as smoke, or tossed into a stream or the ocean. However the prayer sticks are gifted, the prayers you put into them through intent will carry on for some time, transmuted by the powers of fire, water, earth, and air. As an example of their power, Annette and I fashioned prayer sticks from fallen limbs with the intent that we would share our lives, then gave them to a mountain stream—and a few months later we were married.

Protection

It is sometimes necessary to protect yourself from negative energy sent your way, or a psychic attack. In such situations it doesn't matter how powerful the perpetrators seem to be, since the Creator's power makes their efforts ineffectual. This is because when people use negative energy it is all ego related and therefore of limited power. So by summoning as much personal power as possible—by simply being present, grounded and centered—and then asking your power animals, guides, angels, and the Powers to come to your aid, you can protect yourself.

Most human beings are in fact constantly protected by their angels and power animals, and every individual has the ability to open and shut the doors to negative energy. One way sorcerers, witches, and others with evil intent operate is by tricking you into believing they already have control over you. When you take their "hook," believing them, you open the doors to their influence. Since you have free will, your guides and angels will not stop you from taking action, even if it's wrong action.

The "doorway" to allowing negativity in is fear and resistance. If you are fearful of such persons or entities, you energetically establish a connection with them, "feeding" them. By contrast, love, light, and laughter are painful to them, especially if you laugh at them. And indeed, compared to the powers of the universe and the Creator, they are pitiful and laughable, however powerful or fear provoking they may seem.

It is therefore important to remember that all negative energy sent your way is powerless unless it finds a portal into your psyche through fear and resistance. An analogy might be how you would respond after having a handful of angry bees thrown at you. If you acknowledge them, are fearful of them, and swat at them, they will be more prone to attack you. But just as a beekeeper uses smoke to calm bees, you can use prayers, power objects such as crystals, or supplicating to your power animals and the Creator to protect you from negativity's invasion of your being and your home environment. Carrying a photo, drawing, or other representation of your power animals in your pocket or purse can remind you to maintain your connection with the Powers for reassurance and guidance no matter what type of energy comes your way.

Simple Ceremony:
Programming Home Protection

A simple ceremony to protect your home against both directed and unintentional negative energy is to place crystals that have been programmed for protection on each windowsill of your home. After obtaining enough crystals, which can be less than an inch long, program each one and place it on a windowsill. To program the crystal, place it in your left hand, feel your heart energy, and direct feelings of love and protection into the crystal. (You always program a crystal with the left hand and access its information or direct the programmed energy with the right hand.)

If crystals aren't available, cedar can be used for protection. Gather cedar—either fallen wood or small limbs from trees—in a sacred manner, asking permission of the tree and explaining what it will be used for, leaving tobacco or cornmeal in return. Then place the cedar pieces in strategic places around the house, such as on windowsills or over doorways. Because cedar affects anyone carrying negative vibrations, you can hide a piece of cedar near your front door and, by observing who acts nervous around it, determine potential sources of negativity.

If you have already been "tricked" by fear and have allowed yourself to be energetically affected, you can heal any damage done by first immediately reinforcing your circle of protection through the use of crystals or cedar, smudging the interior of your home with sage or cedar smoke, walking four times around your house sprinkling tobacco, cornmeal, or orange peels as a barrier. Next, go inside your house and drum or meditate, asking your power animals to protect you and reclaim the positive energy that was taken. While drumming or meditating, reach out with your intents to connect your home to the Christ Consciousness Grid (often called by native people the plume of *Quetzalcoatl*), and thus raise its vibrational rate. Do not respond whatsoever to any person or entity attacking, as this would only give them energy. Instead, use prayers to deflect negative energy. Further, ask your power animals to erect mirrors around you and your house, to reflect back, with the added vibration of healing, whatever energy is sent your way.

Staffs, Wands, Feathers, Fans, and Rattles

Shamans and other medicine people frequently use staffs, wands, feathers, fans, and rattles in ceremony or for focusing power and intent.

Staffs are generally not utilized in group ceremony but are for personal use to connect with earth and sky and tend to reflect a person's animal totems or other spirit beings. Staffs are very personal objects, for the wood is carefully selected, often intricately carved and decorated with such items as fur and feathers to honor protectors and power animals. They have their own power that works in harmony with the holder, even at a distance. In the hands of a shaman, a staff functions as the tree of life, connecting to everything. Since staffs are not used in ceremony, however, they should be left where the ceremonial elder has designated when entering a ceremonial area. To place a staff within a gathering's circle or outside a tepee, lodge, or living space unless the area is specifically set aside for that purpose is a claim of possession and considered offensive. One should never be left unattended in a public place except to protect personal space, for example, where an individual is sleeping.

Wands may be used in personal ceremony, such as receiving and sending energy for healing or protecting an area. Some crystals function as wands, shaped by their crystalline structure to send and receive energy. A wand is easily made by finding a hollow reed, such as bamboo or cane, and inserting a small crystal in its tip.

Feathers also are frequently used as wands, connecting earth and sky. Each bird has its own qualities, or medicine, determining the choice of feathers for wands. For example, blue herons are powerful healers, reflecting the healing energy of water; vultures (called "peace eagles," because they are the only meat eaters that don't kill to survive) are associated with transformation; eagles fly high, see far, and are considered messengers for the Creator, so medicine people often use eagle feathers in healing ceremonies or for blessings and guidance. It should be noted that in the United States possession of eagle feathers is prohibited under federal law except for members of federally recognized tribes and even then possession is regulated. To avoid legal entanglements, most people who use feathers in ceremony employ feathers of domestic turkeys (often called "ground eagles," because they are premier on the land, far seeing, quick, and elusive, and considered warrior birds that bring abundance).

Fans, ceremonial objects associated with prayer, are used frequently by women and are usually fashioned from colored feathers and beautifully beaded. Additionally, some ornate collapsible fans are used by both men and women in Native American Church ceremonies. In most public ceremonies, women hold a fan and have a shawl draped over one arm, the positioning of which reveals the women's marital status. Moreover, the fan itself is a form of prayer; by holding fans to their hearts, women provide centering for a ceremony to amplify its power. In addition, fans or bird wings are often employed by healers to brush negativity and potential harmful energies from people. In ceremony, the bird wing is often used for bathing participants entering the sacred circle with sage smoke, and in spiritual dances "wing men" may keep the participants bathed in sacred smoke so negativity doesn't attach to the dancers. Native American healers and spiritual leaders of the past have often been pictured in photographs holding their wings, a mark of their role and status within the community.

Rattles used in ceremony may be gourds with the seeds left inside, gourds with pebbles or small crystals added, or even empty plastic soft drink or water bottles with pebbles inside. Rattles are frequently used to shatter existing energy patterns so that a new, higher vibration may be established when creating a sacred circle or before a ceremony begins. Rattles are also used to "call in" spirits, power animals, or soul pieces, depending on the intent and purpose of a ceremony.

Simple Ceremony:
Soul Retrieval by Rattling

Using a rattle to practice soul retrieval is one of the easiest and most powerful ceremonies you can do alone. When trauma occurs, the injury causes a piece of soul essence to be ejected. For example, just before a car crash the driver's consciousness does not want to be present when the person's body collides with the steering wheel, so a piece is ejected at the moment of impact. It is the role of the shaman to go out into nonordinary reality and retrieve the lost piece. In ancient times, indigenous people understood this and whenever people experienced trauma, they were treated immediately for soul loss.[12] When warriors came back from battle, they would avoid contact with the villagers until ceremonies had been held to cleanse them from the bloodshed and retrieve soul pieces lost due to the trauma of war. Soul loss can be experienced for many other reasons as well, such as bad relationships, death of a relationship or loved one, divorce, child abuse, or drug or alcohol abuse, even if the precipitating event occurred decades before.

Symptoms of soul loss include loss of life force, feeling apart from life, feeling depressed or suicidal, being prone to addiction, post-traumatic stress syndrome, excessive grief, or a deep sense that something is missing. The best way to retrieve soul pieces is for a trained practitioner to bring them back, though often such pieces return on their own and hover around the person. In my practice of soul retrieval, I've frequently found that when people start looking for someone to retrieve missing soul pieces, it means some of them have already returned and since lost pieces are often linked, it may take only a little effort and knowledge to get all the remaining pieces to come back, usually by rattling.

To perform soul retrieval by rattling, first create a sacred circle, preferably in a secluded place in nature; ask your guides, angels, and power animals to aid you; and thank them through affirmation for doing so. Next clear your mind, finding your Stillpoint, open yourself, trusting that you are protected, then begin rattling with the intent of calling in missing soul pieces. You may experience odd memories, perhaps related to events of childhood or other incidents too painful to remember. Don't push them away or analyze them, but simply allow the memories to come into consciousness, acknowledge them, and let them go. The missing soul parts coming in are "seating" themselves and pushing out the old, painful memories so healing can occur. After the memories have subsided, stop rattling. Then breathe deeply and cry, laugh, or express any other emotion you feel, releasing all attachment to the past trauma.

Once the rattling is complete, simply let the soul pieces reestablish themselves. Rest and pamper yourself, perhaps taking a long, hot bath, using sea salts or Epsom salts. Because the energetic activity of soul retrieval can cause physiological changes, don't be surprised if you leave a ring around the tub as evidence that old toxins have been released from your body. For the next two or three days, allow plenty of time for reverie. During this time, former talents and interests you may have forgotten about will surface. For example, you might feel the urge to write or paint, or undertake another immersion you gave up years before.

To ensure that these soul pieces do not leave again, it is important that whatever conditions caused them to evacuate are not repeated. This may require a change in attitude or lifestyle, such as stopping drug or alcohol abuse or getting out of an abusive relationship.

From the Energy Notebook: The Pipe, the Drum, and the Staff

On a spirit quest to Black Mesa in the desert region near the border between Oklahoma and New Mexico, I had a revelation about the nature of objects used in ceremony and about possessions in general. Spirit had told me before I left that I should bring all my sacred objects, so I had three medicine bags full. Arriving at the foot of the mountain, I repacked them into one medicine bag I could carry up with me. The day was very hot, about 108 degrees; the bag weighed about forty pounds; and the hike was long. But once I got to the top, unpacked my bag beneath a lone tree, and laid out my sacred objects, I suddenly knew why Spirit had advised me to bring them all.

Gazing at them laid out before me, I saw with great clarity my reason for choosing each object in the first place, what it meant to me, how I had obtained it, and what I used it for. Combined, they amounted to an inventory of my life and everything I held dear, reflecting my hopes, dreams, beliefs, fears, and actions. Each was a symbol of what I carried in my mind, my heart, and my psyche.

Further, I realized that their being a heavy burden to carry up the mountain was part of the lesson. Spirit had in essence told me to look at what I carry around with me and how I use or don't use things, and consider what I truly need and can and cannot let go of. At that moment, I knew I could do without all these things if necessary and that they were but a small portion of the resources available to me. Then there on the mountain the Creator told me, "All you need are your pipe, your drum, and your staff." An eagle cried overhead, making lazy circles in the sky before I heard the voice of the Creator add: "And you don't really need those things. The pipe you carry with you stands for your connection with the Creator, which is always there; your drum stands for the beating of your heart in concert with the Earth Mother, who is always there for you; your staff stands for your beliefs and your faith that all powers of earth and sky are there for you if you will only ask. These are the things that matter and that last."

I laughed, thinking I could have saved myself a lot of exhaustion had I left these material things behind. And yet it was worth the effort to get such a valuable lesson—that we do not need to carry all the things from our past into the future; in fact, we need very few things, all of which are available inside us, waiting only to be discovered in the world around us, if we but open ourselves to perceive them.

Dancing

There are many different types of dances, including those done for fun and fellowship at intertribal powwows, such as the Friendship Dance; those done at tribal ceremonies to connect with nature and Spirit, such as the Buffalo Dance and Deer Dance; and those performed specifically for healing the self and others, such as the shamanic Bear Dance done by the Yokuts, in California. The latter was brought to the people through a vision by Clarence Atwell Sr., who worried about the loss of old ways and the health of his people. Upon the reservation's mountain, the powers showed him the dance and told him to teach it to the people. For the past few years, I have been participating in the Bear Dance, a seven-year commitment to bring healing to the earth and all beings.[13]

In the Bear Dance, dancers "take on" diseases of others and transmute them to effect healing. The dancers must totally become bear energy, so that all disease is taken on by the spirit being of the bear, a dangerous process. The "wing men," those who attend to the bear by using bird wings to whisk away any negative energies that may attach to the dancers, constantly bathe the dancers in sacred sage smoke to help them maintain the bear energy connection free from harm. While they dance, they "are" the bear; the bear spirit takes on all the ills of the people and transmutes that negativity to healing.

Another powerful shamanic dance is the Ghost Dance, which gives participants the ability to connect with the ancestors in Dreamtime—a tremendous spiritual power usually reserved for shamans and holy people. As such, and because of the speed with which it spread through Native America in the nineteenth century, it frightened federal authorities, precipitating the U.S. government massacre at Wounded Knee on December 29, 1890, and the banning of spiritual practices on reservations with severe penalties, until 1978, with passage of the American Indian Religious Freedom Act. The subjugation of such spiritual traditions by native peoples forced most of these practices underground, so that many traditions were lost. The government was threatened by the Ghost Dance because it saw the dance as a way to unite native peoples, and indeed, the dream of many who performed the dance was annihilation of Europeans and a return to the ways that predated their arrival. But the vision of Wovoka, a half-white Northern Paiute who was credited with originating the dance (though it actually originated among the Cherokee), was one of unifying the people spiritually not militarily—a vision of the peaceful unification of native peoples that essentially died at Wounded Knee.[14] Personally, I experienced a related vision in which I saw people dancing the Ghost Dance on a broad plain, with the landscape and the sky both white. It was shown to me that those who danced it would see their way to the next world.

A few days after the vision, I tried the dance, to see if I could remember how I had learned it. As I danced, the weather suddenly turned from clear to overcast, and everything became white, just as in the dream, convincing me that the power of the dance still exists.

Although people have been performing it quietly over the years, friends have warned that it could be dangerous to try to bring it back openly. The late Cherokee medicine man Rolling Thunder, I was reminded, refused to teach it again after he taught it to some non-native people, who then inexplicably died.

This has made me think that due to its associations it may be best if taught only in special circumstances. However, I believe it is time for the Ghost Dance to return, as shown in the vision, and it will help show the way for a better world for all peoples.

There are, however, other shamanic dances that are similar. And many have powerfully positive effects.

Simple Ceremony: Becoming Your Power Animal through Dance

One of the most effective and revealing shamanic dances is to dance your power animal, which can be done anywhere in nature or even in the home. To do this, create a sacred circle and walk the circle while rattling or listening to drumming, either in person or on a CD or tape.[15] Connect with your power animal and allow it to guide you in a dance so that you "become" your power animal, thereby becoming one with this power of the universe. For example, if your power animal is a bird, allow your arms to become its wings and feel yourself soaring, then let the bird reveal insights and wisdom. If you do this ceremony on a regular basis, it will gradually get easier, and your vision will expand, giving healing energy. Keep a journal of your insights so you can continue to learn from them as time passes.

Simple Ceremony: Dance of the Willow

Dance of the Willow can be performed by any individual anywhere, anytime to connect the highest energies within you with the highest energies without. It is a discipline, like tai chi, for moving *ki* energy through the body and also can be viewed as a form of tai chi.

To begin, feel the earth energy coming up through your feet into your body; feel the sky energy coming down through your crown chakra; feel the energies meeting in your heart and going out through your shoulders and arms to your fingertips. Now, extend your arms like a willow tree—out, above, then down, allowing the energies to sway your body, including your limbs, as if caught in a breeze. Move both hands back and forth, imagining a river's waves crossing in front of you, blessing the earth and all beings. Reach up, extending each arm as far as possible; bring your hands around in front of you, about a foot apart; and feel the energy running between them, like a ball. Visualizing the ball of energy, push it out into space, with blessings for all beings, imagining it being absorbed by the Earth Mother and thereby going wherever it might be needed. Finally, return your hands to your sides and give thanks.

Simple Ceremony:
Eye of the Raven Dance

Since we are all of the Earth Mother, any life essence of the Earth belongs to us all and when lost can be found and retrieved by groups of people holding intent in concert with the Powers. Performing prayer through group dance is a way to retrieve lost life essence and return it to the Earth so all may benefit through increased harmony and healing in the world. One such dance, called the Eye of the Raven Ceremony, is for a group of men and women, with a leader who drums. This dance was given to me in vision, though it's very old; it's named after the

Raven as the Power who gives magic and protection, and it reflects the eye of the Raven which is the essence of Creator's sight: two concentric rings going in opposite directions that actually are one; we only see them as two in this world.

To do this ceremony, first form a circle with each person experiencing in their heart the place in the circle that feels most natural. Facing inward, in silence give thanks to the Earth Mother for all she provides—food, shelter, life—and acknowledge that human bodies are made of her elements, along with those of all beings that depend on her for sustenance. Feel a connection with the heart of the Earth Mother.

As the leader begins to drum, turn outward and sit, inviting all the spirits of fire, water, earth, and air to join the circle. Then broaden the invitation to include spirits who are not incarnate but who help guide and teach those who are companions and guardians; ancestors; and descendents, those who have lived on Earth or will some day. All, like us, are stakeholders in the well-being of the Earth Mother.

After these spirits have joined and their presence has been felt, still sitting, turn inward again, and listen with hearts open to each spirit voice speaking. Once all the spirits have spoken, thank them for having participated and, still in silence, join them in prayer, asking the Creator to hear their prayer, that essence belonging to the earth be returned for the good of all beings in the world.

As you pray, plant a prayer stick in the ground for all beings past, present, and future, the stakeholders of this earth. After all the sticks are planted, form two circles, women on the outside, men on the inside. Then dance (clockwise for women, counterclockwise for men) accompanied by drumming and singing, asking that each help each other call in any life essence that belongs to the Earth for healing and wholeness.

Finally, as the leader gives a drumroll, form one circle holding hands and give thanks to the Creator and the Earth Mother for this moment of standing between earth and sky with all relations as one voice. Then embrace one another, sharing hearts.

Walking in Prayer

Walking in prayer is an effective means of connecting with Spirit and the powers of nature, especially when traveling across sacred land forms, such as a sacred mountain or valley. While walking in prayer, I have come upon napping deer and feeding rabbits that were unafraid and carried on without noticeably moving. If done barefoot in the dark, walking in prayer can put you in a more intense dreamlike state in which union with the landscape seems a constant reality. Sometimes for guidance and prayer I go to a sacred mountain at night and walk barefoot up the trail, feeling the Earth energy through my feet and "seeing" not by the light of day but with inner light. In this dreamlike state, my senses are so acute that sight is unnecessary; unable to see the boundaries *between* objects, I can more easily merge and feel one with all living things.

In this state, I also experience timelessness more easily, minutes seeming like hours or vice versa, each moment eternal. At dawn I stop and watch the sun rise over the valley below, whatever troubles I had gone or burned away by a new sun rising.

Simple Ceremony:
The Power Walk and the Listening Walk

There are two simple ways to walk in prayer, depending on the circumstances. One way, called a Power Walk, is to hold your prayer stick in one hand and a rattle in the other, rattling as you go along, according to intent, fast for breaking up energy, slow for calling in spirits. The prayer stick focuses your attention on the present and indicates to the spirits of the land that you are walking in Spirit. Allow your intuition, guides, and angels to show you where to go so you have every opportunity for encountering a form of Spirit or learning through the journey.

The second way to walk in prayer, called a Listening Walk, is to slip silently through the landscape like a ghost. Walk slowly, pausing often to connect with everything around you, wordlessly like a bird that glides on the winds, slowing here, speeding up there, merging with the airstream. In this way, your feet kiss the Earth Mother, and you become one with her, the movements as of the gentle wind, your awareness one with all beings, all your relations. It is a living prayer with the earth and sky.

Singing

Singing is one of the most sacred practices you can perform, either alone in nature or in a group. The voice has great power when expressing love from the heart. The ability of sound to induce meditative states was known thousands of years ago to ancient Hindu and Buddhist cultures, which used rhythmic chanting, singing bowls, finger chimes, and other methods to transcend ordinary consciousness. Many people believe that sacred songs must be learned from others by repetition, but although that's a good practice, such songs are not any more sacred than using your own voice, the voice the Creator has given you, with positive intention.

In the old days, people would go out in nature and allow the Creator to give them heart songs, sacred songs that had meaning for them and that were often used in family ceremonies, some of which continue to survive.[16] It should be noted that some of these songs were so sacred that if one person heard another singing them, they would demand an explanation of how the songs were obtained and for what purpose; to determine who had given the song, or if it were stolen. Whole tribes actually went to war over songs that were stolen, or not given and received in the right way. Consequently, when singing a sacred song, it is advisable to announce who taught it to you and for what purpose, whether it was learned from a person, CD, or tape. This practice honors the origin and maintains the tradition and power of the song.

For example, one of my teachers, Doc Chanter Davidson, an Apache who follows the Yokuts way, gave a song, called in English, "Women's Eagle Song" to Annette that belonged to a Yokuts woman who outlived her eight children and five husbands and attributed her longevity to the song. Knowing the origin and purpose of the song gives it a special meaning for us, and when my wife sings it in the lodge or under her breath at home, I laugh, wondering if she is planning on outliving me. But I take great joy in hearing her sing it as its intention is positive and hopeful for the future. Another song, which we call "Yaki-Yaki," was given to both of us by my Choctaw shaman friend Boe Many Knives Glasschild, whose grandfather was Blackfeet (mother and grandmother Choctaw, another grandmother Cherokee).[17] It's a Blackfeet creation or wedding song that we have adopted as "our song." Wherever we go, we sing it from the heart together, delighting others, and we frequently sing it when I am called to perform weddings.

A healing song we sing only in special circumstances at Bear Lodge is composed simply of the words *Ona, Yona, Elohino*—Cherokee words for Creator, Bear, Earth Mother. Another healing song consists simply of one word, *U-halo-tega*, Creator, source of all power, repeated. Although the words have meaning, it's how they are sung, the heartfelt intent, that ultimately gives them power and affects healing.

Simple Ceremony:
Creating Sacred Songs

To discover your own sacred songs, go into nature and make a sacred circle then listen to everything around and inside you, to all the sounds of life and to your own heart. Listen carefully to the birds and animals, the sounds of the wind through the trees, and see what "comes up" into your consciousness. What words come forward? They don't need to make rational sense, only that they fit the feelings and insights you obtain. Play with the tones and inflections of words, varying them. The song will soon attain a life of its own and seem to be one with the Creator's power. To create such sacred songs is empowering, and then to pass them on to others is a great gift.

Drumming

Native Americans and most other indigenous peoples of the world have known for thousands of years that drumming is a powerful spiritual tool. Only in recent years, however, has the scientific basis for this come to light—the beat of the drum used to transport native peoples into shamanic states of consciousness, about 180 cycles per second, closely approximates the base resonant frequency of the Earth itself. Thus drumming becomes a powerful meditation tool, as well as a way to tap into our psychic ability to travel over vast distances to effect cures and to know and affect the future.

Through shamanic journeying using the drum, we can travel along our energy field lines through dimensions—in ordinary three-dimensional reality, or the nonordinary "middle world," or anywhere on Earth or in other universes, thereby experiencing "visualized prayer."[18] In addition, other benefits of drumming are reduction of stress through balancing the chakras and a creative alternative to "zoning out" after work in front of the television. Learning to journey is an invaluable way to access the world of healing and can be learned by anyone with supervision or by using the many books and tapes available on the subject.

Simple Ceremony:
Balancing Chakras with the Drum

Lie down and slowly roll a small hand drum, about 13 inches in diameter or less, from your abdomen to your forehead, while beating the drum and noticing how its tone varies as it rolls across your body. This is an indication that the chakras, or energy centers, in your body are out of balance, especially likely after a stressful day. To balance your chakras, continue to roll the drum slowly up and down your body, while beating it softly and steadily until the pitch of the drum remains constant as it is moved and you feel less stressful and more relaxed.

Drum Circle

A great way to do ceremony in groups, either in the home or in nature, is by forming a drum circle to meet regularly to drum together. Drum circles usually are small and composed of individuals who like to journey shamanically together. We began our drum circle in the year 2000, calling it the New Millennium Drum Circle, with the hope of using it in the new century for drumming to heal and balance ourselves, others, and the Earth. Its formation coincided with the creation of the Web site Healing the Earth/Ourselves (http://www.blueskywaters.com/) and the monthly e-mail newsletter that now goes out across the United States and to several countries overseas. The drum circle arose out of our practice of sponsoring workshops for the Foundation for Shamanic Studies. For the past six years we have met, with the number of participants varying from a dozen to forty-seven, but the upstairs of our small house can comfortably seat only thirty. We now limit the group to that number, and any additional participants drum downstairs with an electronic baby monitor so all people are synchronized.

Although drum circles tend to limit participants to those with shamanic training,[19] ours does not but is held in two sessions: the first, at 5:30 p.m., is for those with shamanic training, while the second, at 7:00 p.m., is for those without it. The first session focuses on journeying together and discussing any problems that come up, while the second session emphasizes use of the Native American medicine wheel for prayers and healing, honoring each of the directions with four rounds of drumming. It is a prayer ceremony open to everyone. A key element of the round honoring south is passing a prayer stick so that each person can speak from the heart in prayer. In this way, all voices are heard with respect. We also have a prayer basket in the medicine wheel for people who have submitted prayers to be included in the ceremony.

In the medicine wheel drum circle prayer ceremony, people have had visions resulting in major life changes, such as seeking counseling for drug or alcohol abuse, leaving bad relationships, or taking risks to try new ones. The ceremony's power derives from the fact that it raises the vibrational level of the whole group, whose prayers and energy go outward, healing the Earth and all beings. As one rather surprised Lakota visitor, who had been skeptical before attending, said afterwards, "It's like a sweat lodge without the sweat!"

People routinely travel many miles to participate in this ceremony, coming from surrounding states and even, on occasion, foreign countries. The fact that our drum circle in Lena, Mississippi, population 289, is open to people of so many different beliefs and from such a variety of places—including Arkansas, Louisiana, Tennessee, and Alabama, as well as Brazil, Colombia, Mexico, and Japan—adds to the power of prayer during ceremony. Frequently, people around the world will join at the time we drum, adding their voices and prayers to the ceremonies. We've also taken the drum circle across America, performing ceremonies from Miami to Los Angeles, at which people of every race, creed, and national origin have joined in, including Christians, Muslims, Jews, and Buddhists. A high wiccan priest became one of our regulars, once saying afterwards, "Here I find peace." In addition to opening our doors to everyone, we encourage those who have turned their backs on religion and young people searching for a path to find Spirit in their lives. The philosophy behind the drum circle stems from the words of Jesus "In My Father's house are many mansions." We add the credo "All doors lead to the same room."

As a result of the drum circle's popularity, others like it have sprung up elsewhere—extensions we've encouraged. People all around the world have written to find out how to start one. The following instructions include the basic steps.

Simple Ceremony:
Drum Circle

Invite your friends over who have positive intent for healing. It does not matter if the drum circle is large or small, the secret to its power is intent and commitment. The ceremony is conducted not only for the people present but for the Earth and all beings.

Begin by creating a sacred circle using five stones, either indoors or out. Use the medicine wheel for prayers and healing, honoring each of the directions with four rounds of drumming (See: "Welcoming The Powers of the Directions," Chapter 1). When honoring the south, pass a prayer stick so each person can speak a prayer from the heart. Continue to make prayers for all people and the Earth, ensuring that all voices are heard, calling on the powers to help, and giving supplications then thanks.

It is a good thing if all who attend bring food to share, so that fellowship and feasting can occur afterwards. That sharing, love, and friendship is as important as the ceremony itself.

Notes

Preface

1. See Looking Back Woman's Web site:
    http://www.lookingbackwoman.com.

2. Mails, Thomas E. *Fools Crow* (Lincoln, NE: University of
    Nebraska Press, 1990). Fools Crow also stated: "The ones
    who complain and talk the most about giving away
    Medicine Secrets, are always those who know the least."

    The need for ever more human beings to discover and
    practice ways of spiritual power is ever greater day by day.
    In recent years, Gregg Braden, a geophysicist and author of
    Awakening to Zero Point: The Collective Initiation (Bellevue,
    WA: Radio Bookstore Press, 1997) and *Walking Between the
    Worlds: The Science of Compassion* (Bellevue, WA: Radio
    Bookstore Press, 1997), has hypothesized that the Earth is
    going through great changes with profound implications
    for its inhabitants, coinciding with ancient prophecies of
    the Egyptians, Hopi, Aztecs, and Mayans, as well as those
    found in the Christian Bible.

    As Dhyani Ywahoo, a Cherokee (Tsalagi) teacher, explains
    in her book, *Voices of the Ancestors: Cherokee Teachings from
    the Wisdom Fire:* "Through prayer and ritual the stability of
    the physical form is maintained. In this time, right action
    is being called forth from all, to renew The Sacred Hoop. As
    sacred ceremonies are kept, dances danced, the lunar and
    solar currents within the individual clearly resonate with
    the lunar and solar energies of the planet. As individuals
    maintain attitudes of alienation and ideas of domination
    over the natural order of things and over one another,
    there occurs an obstruction of the flow among the
    individual, the group, and the electromagnetic current of
    the Earth, thereby disturbing the flow of the wind and the
    lightning, which brings life-giving rain and germination
    properties to the seed. Hence, each one is called to make a
    choice: with the stream or not. No equivocation."

Notes

In 1969, her Sunray Meditation Society was founded as a
vehicle for the appropriate teachings of the Ywahoo
lineage to be shared with those of one heart, and today
students and practitioners of the Sunray teachings are
flourishing as seeds of light and right relationship in
communities throughout Turtle Island (North America) and
the world. See her Web site: http://www.sunray.org.

In all wisdom traditions, there is a vast divide between
overt and covert Spirit and knowledge—between the
outward form we call religion and Spirit knowledge *behind*
the religion. For example, when one enters a church, the
objects and ritual are fairly predictable, but the covert
expressions of Spirit include doctrinal teachings that can be
learned only during years of study. Throughout history,
priestly castes have used the covert form of spiritual
knowledge to gain or maintain power and to assert
authority over entire populations. This has happened in
Western, Eastern, and New World cultures, from Egyptian
pharaohs to the Roman Church to the Inca Empire.

Additionally, some spiritual leaders, including many
medicine men and shamans, have kept their knowledge
covert because it adds to the sense of mystery and power
associated with them. Knowledge is power, and fear and
ignorance are powerful tools to keep "common" people in
their place.

The path of a true teacher and of Spirit, however, is to
reveal the hidden, to open the way for emanations of love
and light, making the world a brighter, more enlivened and
loving place. The Creator creates abundance in all things,
in all ways, eternally; the Creator doesn't restrict
expression, hide knowledge, or provoke fear. These are
instead the protocols of people with closed hearts who
want to *hold* power, not *know* power.

True power is in beings greater than ourselves. We want to
be as hollow bones, allowing the Creator's power to come
through us uninhibited, without ego getting in the way.
Those who seek to hold the sacred teachings covert, to
make them occult, are doing themselves and humankind

153

no good. Those who stand for light will illuminate the way, and no amount of casting dark words or thoughts will harm them, for their words will resonate, and the people who hear them will feel the light of the Creator within them, the good medicine (or, in Cherokee, *nvwati*).

3. See http://www.whitebison.org White Bison is a marvelous organization that has helped many people maintain sobriety, although its daily meditations (sent via e-mail to subscribers' mailboxes free of charge) is helpful for anyone following the spiritual path in the Native American way. It was founded by Don Coyhis, a member of the Mohican Nation from the Stockbridge-Munsee Reservation in Wisconsin. Since 1988, he has developed and presented programs based on the teachings of the Medicine Wheel and a system of principles, values, and laws that were given to him by Native American Elders.

4. Boyd, Doug. *Mad Bear: Spirit, Healing, and the Sacred in the Life of a Native American Medicine Man* (New York: Touchstone, 1994).

5. Catches, Pete S., Sr., Peter V. Catches, ed. *Sacred Fireplace (Oceti Wakan): Life and Teachings of a Lakota Medicine Man* (Santa Fe, NM: Clear Light Publishers, 1999).

6. See http://www.lookingbackwoman.com.

Chapter One

1. For more information on Toltec shamanism, see books by Carlos Castaneda, such as *The Teachings of Don Juan: A Yaqui Way of Knowledge* (New York: Ballantine, 1969); books by Don Miguel Ruiz, such as *The Four Agreements* (San Rafael, CA: Amber-Allen Publishing, 1997); and Ken Eagle Feather's *A Toltec Path* (Charlottesville, VA: Hampton Roads, 1995). Because of the popularity of these teachings, approaching reality from this perspective has become a form of consensus reality among many people and, therefore, is easy to access.

2. For more information about Coyote, see Jamie Sams, *Dancing the Dream: The Seven Sacred Paths of Human*

Transformation (New York: HarperCollins, 1998) and
Christopher Moore, *Coyote Blue* (New York: HarperCollins,
2004). Sams' book gives excellent teachings on the
medicine wheel, including how Coyote comes in to mess
up our plans and ideas. Moore's book is about having
Coyote as a power animal, or spirit guide, and the types of
tricks he plays, suggesting that having Coyote as your
power animal may not be advantageous—unless you want
to invite the old Chinese curse "May your life be
interesting."

3.   This technique, called the Gassho Meditation, is taught by
William Lee Rand, founder of the International Center for
Reiki Training. Although it is not discussed in this book, I
encourage individuals to explore Reiki, which is a powerful
way of healing using the hands. For more information,
contact the International Center for Reiki Training, 21421
Hilltop Street, Unit #28, Southfield, MI 48034; phone: 800-
332-8112; Web site: http://www.reiki.org.

Chapter Two

1.   See John G. Neihardt, *Black Elk Speaks: Being the Life Story of
a Holy Man of the Oglala Sioux* (Lincoln: University of
Nebraska Press, 2000).

2.   See David Bohm, *Wholeness and the Implicate Order* (Boston:
Routledge & Kegan Paul, 1980).

3.   See Maureen J. Kelly, *Reiki and the Healing Buddha* (Twin
Lakes, WI: Lotus Press, 2000).

4.   See the late Ian Xel Lungold's Web site:
http://www.mayanmajix.com, featuring his *Mayan Calendar
and Conversion Codex* (Sedona, AZ: Majix Inc., 1999), which
I use daily; also *Healing the Earth/Ourselves*
(http://www.blueskywaters.com): "The Mayan Calendar: A
Roadmap to Consciousness."

5.   See Drunvalo Melchizedek's books *Ancient Secrets of the
Flower of Life,* vols. 1 and 2 (Flagstaff, AZ: Light Technology
Publishing, 1990), which are taught in courses given by
Flower of Life Research LLC, P.O. Box 55844, Phoenix, AZ

85078; phone: 602-996-0900; Web site: http://
www.floweroflife.org. The books and courses are both
highly recommended. In sacred geometry, two particularly
meaningful concepts are the golden mean spiral and the
Fibonacci spiral. The Fibonacci spiral is the mathematical
formula for all forms on earth, for example, in a snail's
shell and in the pattern of leaves on a plant. The golden
mean spiral is the infinite ideal, which in mathematics has
no beginning and no end but is a continuous number (the
sequence of the pi ratio: 1.6180339...). When the golden
mean spiral comes into this plane, it is translated into a
three-dimensional form, which is the Fibonacci spiral. The
golden mean spiral can be seen as coming from a plane
below this one and expressing itself on this plane in the
natural, physical shapes of all things, by using its three-
dimensional form, the Fibonacci spiral, then spiraling on
to the next plane. From the Fibonacci spiral, the one—the
circle, dot, point, or doorway—is derived all material forms:
the sphere, the dodecahedron, the icosahedron, the
octahedron, the hexahedron, and the tetrahedron, the
basic forms found in nature around us all the time.

Regarding seeing duality as one, as the Creator does, rather
than as polarity, which we are accustomed to doing, there
are many examples we can point to. The earth itself reflects
the simultaneous clockwise and counterclockwise
movement; for example, in the Northern Hemisphere
water naturally swirls clockwise, while in the Southern
Hemisphere it swirls counterclockwise. The Creator sees the
unity of both; we discern differences. Doing ceremony
clockwise in the Southern Hemisphere does not negate the
ceremony but merely mirrors that done in the Northern
Hemisphere. The oldest Cherokee dances, for example, are
counterclockwise because, it's believed, the original peoples
came from the Southern Hemisphere and carried their
ceremonies with them—which does not detract from their
power. Further, although the circle of creation appears to
go clockwise, or sunwise, which is how most sacred
ceremonies are conducted, it actually goes clockwise and
counterclockwise at once. By way of explanation, in using

the medicine wheel it aids in seeing polarities as one, as the Creator would, by imagining the circle actually being concentric rings so close together they appear as one, going in opposite directions at the same time—so, when doing ceremony, one moves outward (clockwise), sending prayers throughout the universe, while the other moves inward, connecting prayers to the Source.

Chapter Three

1. For more information about land forms, see my book *Clearing: A Guide for Liberating Energies Trapped in Buildings and Lands,* illustrated by Annette Waya Ewing, with a foreword by Brooke Medicine Eagle (Findhorn, Scotland: Findhorn Press, 2006).

2. Exercises 5 and 6 were taught by the late Debra Harrison, who with Dr. Mary A. Lynch formed a wellness model through Consegrity Inc., that is no longer in business. The wellness model, however, continues as Consilience; see http:// www.energymirrors.com.

3. Similar meditations are provided by William Lee Rand and the International Center for Reiki Training (http:// www.reiki.org) and Brian Weiss, M.D., *Messages from the Masters* (New York: Warner Books, 2000) and *Many Lives, Many Masters* (New York: Fireside, 1988); also Dr. Andrew Weil, including *Dr. Andrew Weil's Mindbody Toolkit: Experience Self Healing with Clinically Proven Techniques* (Audio CD).

Chapter Four

1. The ability to transmute energy in a substance, particularly water, through intent has been well documented by Japanese researcher Masaru Emoto. See his books, *The Message from Water,* vols. 1 and 2 (Tokyo, Japan: Hado Kyoikusha, 2004), or visit his Web site at http://www.masaru-emoto.net.

2. This is separate from the Cherokee sacred way, which is known as the White Path, or the way toward the divine.

Similarly, the Iroquois notion of the White Roots of Peace, which promotes the good mind or right thinking, is in its own way worthy of emulation. Although following the Red Road, thereby choosing unity instead of division, has become a positive pan-Indian concept, accepted across tribes or nations, many Native Americans today seem to have little idea of its meaning and choose division while claiming to follow the Red Road. But following the Red Road is a choice each individual must make, regardless of race or culture; one isn't born following the right path or in any way entitled to it; and the fruits of one's life—tolerance, respect, compassion, and forgiveness, or intolerance, criticism, harsh judgment, proving oneself "right," and holding grudges—clearly reflect the road each individual is following.

3. For more about raising the vibrational rates of land forms, see my book *Clearing: A Guide for Liberating Energies Trapped in Buildings and Lands,* illustrated by Annette Waya Ewing, with a foreword by Brooke Medicine Eagle (Findhorn, Scotland: Findhorn Press, 2006).

4. Shoshone spiritual elder Bennie Blue Thunder LeBeau has been conducting giant medicine wheel ceremonies in the western United States for earth healing. It was my honor to be an ambassador (elder conducting ceremonies) for his 600-Mile Medicine Wheel ceremony in 2004, and he has continued his work in various locales. His Web site is: http://www.teton-rainbows.com.

5. Another valuable resource for healing lands and waters are the classes offered by Sandra Ingerman based on her book *Medicine for the Earth: How to Transform Personal and Environmental Toxins.* You may write to obtain a schedule of her Medicine for the Earth workshops at P.O. Box 4757, Santa Fe, NM 87502. Or visit her Web site: http://www.shamanicvisions.com.

6. See "The Protection of Ceremonies" on the Web site Healing the Earth/Ourselves, http://www.blueskywaters.com.

7. Symbols can take many forms and each have power. For example, the basic shapes of sacred geometry—the sphere, the dodecahedron, the icosahedron, the octahedron, the hexahedron—each have qualities that bring in higher vibrations. A number of Native American symbols have Power and are universal; for example, Golden Eagle, formerly known as Standing Elk, a member of the Dakota Ihunktowan Band of South Dakota, a spiritual elder, and one of the seven Sundance Chiefs of the Yankton Sioux, has co-authored the book *Maka Wicahpi Wicohan,* available along with symbols and explanations on his Web site: http://www.star-knowledge.net/. Here in Lena, we often use an ancient healing symbol called the Antahkarana, as well as incorporate The Alphabet of the Star Beings (Dolphins & Whales). For more information, see the Web site: Healing The Earth/Ourselves, http://www.blueskywaters.com

8. For ceremonies along these lines, including personal empowerment for women, I highly recommend two books by Brooke Medicine Eagle: *The Last Ghost Dance: A Guide for Earth Mages* (New York: Wellspring/Ballantine, 2000) and *Buffalo Woman Comes Singing* (New York: Ballantine Books, 1991). Brooke is the creator of Eagle Song, a series of spiritually oriented wilderness camps, and the FlowerSong Earth Wisdom Institute, which promotes a sustainable, ecologically sound path upon earth for seven generations of children. See her Web site: http://www.medicine-eagle.com. Also, see the Web site of Kathleen Spider Lawrence, a wisdomkeeper and a teacher of Earth connection following the Taino tradition of the Caney Indian Spiritual Circle and the Wisdom Wheel teachings of the Seneca Wolf Clan Teaching Lodge, who has written articles and given lectures internationally about moon time for women: http://www.healing-arts.org/spider. For historical fiction about such practices in biblical times, see Anita Diamant, The Red Tent (New York: St. Martin's Press, 1997).

9. See note 1, chapter 2, Black Elk, et al.

10. I support the Keepers of the Sacred Tradition of Pipemakers, which will quarry the stone and fashion pipes for sale; see http://www.pipekeepers.org. The *chanunpa* and the stone are sacred, but it is not useful to cloud the issue by saying one group is right and all others are wrong. It is a wrong use of power to try to manipulate and control spiritual beliefs and practices. Tribal people have been trading stones and pipes for centuries. Travis Erickson and Bud Johnston are honorable people who do things in a good way; Erickson is a fourth-generation quarrier of the Sisseton-Wahpeton tribe who has been quarrying at Pipestone for more than thirty years and does the work in a sacred manner.

11. See Peter V. Catches Jr.'s Web site: http://www.ocetiwakan.org. He has written a book, *Sacred Fireplace: Life and Teachings of a Lakota Medicine Man* (Santa Fe, NM: Clear Light Publishing, 1999), and a Lakota language book and CD sold on his Web site to fund his charitable work. Catches (Zintkala Oyate), a descendent of thirty-seven generations of medicine men, is Keeper of the Spotted Eagle Way of Lakota medicine, its oral history, sacred rites, and experiential teachings. He has conducted the Spotted Eagle Sun Dance at his home on the Pine Ridge Reservation in South Dakota for twenty-eight consecutive years.

12. See books by Sandra Ingerman: *Soul Retrieval: Mending the Fragmented Self* (San Francisco: Harper, 1991) and *Welcome Home: Following Your Soul's Journey Home* (San Francisco: Harper, 1993). For more information on shamanic journeys, the Foundation for Shamanic Studies teaches a Basic Shamanism class, as well as advanced training. The foundation is a nonprofit international educational organization dedicated to the preservation and teaching of shamanic knowledge for the welfare of the planet and its inhabitants. It is a 501(c)(3) public charitable organization; contributions are tax deductible as allowed by law. Scholarship rebates are available to Native Americans on tribal rolls for all FSS workshops. Contact the Foundation for Shamanic Studies, P.O. Box 1939, Mill Valley, CA

94942; phone 415-380-8282; Web site
http://www.shamanism.org. Also, check for workshops at
Omega, at http:// www.omega.org, or Alberto Villoldo's
Four Winds Society at http://www.thefourwinds.org.

13. I dance with the Bear Society of Russellville, Arkansas. The
schedule is usually posted on the Web site Healing the
Earth/Ourselves, http://www.blueskywaters.com.

14. It should be noted that twenty Congressional Medals of
Honor were awarded to soldiers participating in the
Wounded Knee Massacre in which 290 overwhelmingly
unarmed mostly elderly men, women, and children were
killed. Wovoka died as Jack Wilson in 1932, after playing
bit parts in silent movie westerns and as a sideshow
attraction. To read more about the unholy treatment of
Native Americans and its effects, see *Native American
Spirituality: Freedom Denied* or *Blood Quantum: Native
America's Dirty Little Secret* on the Web site, Healing the
Earth/Ourselves, http:// www.blueskywaters.com.

15. CDs are available on the Web site, Healing the
Earth/Ourselves, http://www.blueskywaters.com, as well as
on the Foundation for Shamanic Studies site, http://
www.shamanism.org; also, Sandra Ingerman's book
Shamanic Journeying: A Beginner's Guide (Boulder, CO:
Sounds True, 2004) includes a drumming CD.

16. CDs are available on the Web site, Healing the
Earth/Ourselves, http://www.blueskywaters.com; also, Peter
V. Catches Jr., a thirty-eighth generation Lakota Sioux
medicine man, has sacred songs and a CD in the Lakota
language book he sells on his Web site:
http://www.ocetiwakan.org.

17. Boe Many Knives Glasschild's "Lightning Dance" teachings
are available at: http://www.creatrixstudio.com. His e-book,
The Shores Within, can be ordered at
http://www.manataka.org/page882.html.

18. See note 12.

19. For a listing of drum circles nationally and internationally,
see http://www.shamaniccircles.org/.

Glossary

allies. Wild spirits of the land that can aid in healing and protecting natural habitats.

all-time, no-time. The present, accessed at its deepest level.

angels. Emissaries of light of divine origin who accompany humans through life and are available for assistance and inspiration.

animus. The spark of life.

archetypes. Attributes existing in potential form that can be brought into manifestation; original models after which other similar things are patterned.

ascension. Transcending to a higher level of consciousness; the next step in human and planetary evolution.

aura. Perceived emanations of the energy body, often seen as colors that show moods, thoughts, or potentials; energetic fields surrounding the physical body, including physical, etheric, emotional, mental, astral, etheric template, celestial, and causal.

authentic self. Who you really are, not who you think you are, or have been told you are by outside sources.

centering. Locating the core of consciousness in the body; drawing magnetic energy from the earth and electrical energy from the sun to operate with balanced awareness.

chakra. Sanskrit for circle or wheel; the energetic centers in the core of the body linked together by a central psychic energy channel.

Christ Consciousness Grid (also called the Plume of Quetzalcoatl). An energy layer surrounding the Earth that signifies the Earth's highest potential established by higher beings, often referred to as ascended beings, or Powers, or Holy Ones, to help humanity through the current "shift of the ages."

cleansing. Transmuting energy to a higher, more positive form by raising its vibrational rate.

clearing. Dissipating (transmuting) negative energy. Clearing spaces usually also cleanses them since the act of clearing raises the vibrational rate.

cocreating. Operating as a partner with the Creator.

ego. The survival mechanism, which is part of the personality. See personality.

energy. Subtle power manifested through life force, frequency, or cohesion.

energy body. A body that exists beyond the physical plane; in humans, such a body extends twenty-seven feet in each direction and thereafter continues into other dimensions. See aura.

fast. See vision quest.

flow of creation. The movement or stasis of energy in a given moment arising from the beginning of the world and continuing through time.

God vs. Creator. God is one, all; the Creator is the active aspect of God as expressed in the will of creation.

goddesses. Land spirits of the highest order, usually associated with a place or characteristic; also, humans who have transcended but chosen to remain on Earth in spirit form as a means of service.

grounding. Connecting with the Earth energetically to ensure that consciousness is not operating from other dimensions or overly affected by other energetic forces.

guides. Spirit helpers, soul brothers or sisters from former or future lifetimes, or spiritual masters or beings who have assumed a supportive role for a particular soul's evolution.

heart song, or power song. A song that expresses the unique, positive energies, traits, and intents of an individual, usually discovered through fasting and prayer.

higher power. God as expressed through one's highest nature.

kachinas. Supernatural beings revered by the Hopi and appearing as messengers from the spirit world; spirit beings.

lela wakan. Lakota term meaning "very sacred."

ley lines. Grids that crisscross the Earth and hold potential electromagnetic energy, many of which were identified by ancient peoples, who built sacred sites over them.

life-force energy. Energy that is all around us in nature and that is emitted by the Earth.

light body. Energetic body; the quality of energy around a person, as opposed to their physical body. See MerKaBa.

matter. Patterns of energy we perceive as having substance.

medicine. The inherent power within all things.

medicine wheel. A Native American system of prayer, meditation, and discovery, recognizing that life follows a circle. The wheel's directions and their significance, concepts from which all things are said to derive, include east (newness, discovery), south (youth, growth, healing), west (introspection, setting sun, light within), north (wisdom, elders, ancestors), center (soul, spirit), above (Heavenly Father), and below (Earth Mother).

meridians. Lines along the body where energy is channeled; often used in acupuncture and other energy medicine to effect healing.

MerKaBa. In sacred geometry, a star tetrahedron; an energetic framework that forms a blueprint for spirit to attach and from which, in plants and animals, DNA creates a physical expression; a geometric form that includes the light body; a pattern of energy shared by animals, plants, stones, and all objects, including those that are man-made.

mind of God. Expansion of human thought to higher consciousness as far as is conceivable.

morphogenic field. A universal field encoding the basic pattern of an object. From the Greek *morphe*, which means form, and *genesis,* which denotes coming into being. Noncorporeal beings manifest in three-dimensional reality through morphogenic resonance.

nagual. In Toltec shamanism, what is really real (nonordinary reality), as opposed to what we think is real according to our consensus reality; everything that can be. See tonal.

native peoples. Indigenous cultures practicing traditional nature-based ways.

nonordinary reality. Reality as seen when everyday constraints and predispositions are eliminated through trance or other methods.

personality. All that we adhere to, or believe, that makes us who we think we are. See ego.

pipe fast. See vision quest.

portal. A vortex through which objects and entities can pass from one dimension of reality to another while realm shifting.

power animal. A power of the universe in animal form that offers guidance and protection; a totem.

power song, or heart song. A song that expresses the unique, positive energies, traits, and intents of an individual, usually discovered through fasting and prayer.

power spot. A place where all energies of a structure or tract of land are focused.

prana. Universal life-force energy.

prayer stick. A stick, either ornate or plain, that has been consecrated through prayer; wrapped with cloth, ribbon, or yarn; used in prayer; often planted in the ground to carry a prayer.

rattling. Shaking a rattle to break up energy or bring in energy.

realm shifting. The movement of objects between dimensions; while some objects, such as quartz crystals, do this routinely because of their energetic composition, others will disappear and reappear only when near a portal.

Reiki. A Japanese form of energy medicine involving sacred symbols and guides; use of the hands to channel healing energy.

sacred circle. All that is revered, held holy, respected; a contained space that is consecrated; family, friends, loved ones as a unit; all beings in our lives—past, present, and future—who are connected to us.

self-talk. The inner dialogue inside our minds; the "what ifs," "buts," judgments, and fears that prevent us from being who we really are.

shaman. Siberian word meaning "one who sees in the dark"; a person who uses Earth energy, guides, and power animals for insight; a medicine man or woman.

shielding. Creating, through intent, a protective energy layer around you to deflect external negative energy.

shift of the ages. Powerful changes in energy patterns now occurring on Earth as a prelude to earth transformations and humanity's eventual development of higher consciousness.

skan. From the Lakota, meaning power of the wind; a sacred force of movement; that which existed before God; life-force energy; the principle that manifests prayers from prayer flags.

smudging. Burning a plant such as sage, cedar, or sweetgrass to purify the energy of an area.

soul. The essential life force, or essence, of a being that is eternal from lifetime to lifetime.

soul retrieval. The act of retrieving soul parts, or essence, lost through trauma or stolen by another individual.

space. Any defined area, including the objects within it.

spiral of ascension. Spiral of life that offers a changing perspective as new lessons are encountered and old ones repeated, until the lessons are finally learned.

spirit. The essential quality of a being as an expression of soul; noncorporeal aspect of a person aligned with soul purpose.

spirit quest. Following only what spirit dictates, usually over the course of days.

star beings. Beings from the stars whom cultures around the globe and throughout time revere as having influenced human development and who are honored at some sacred spots.

Stillpoint. An inner place of total silence and stillness, where intuition and creativity originate and balance can be found; the source of being.

Glossary

thought forms. Organized patterns of energy, either free floating or embedded in a space, that can be broken up by rattling or other means of transmutation.

tonal. In Toltec shamanism, the idea of what is real (our common, consensus reality), in contrast to what is really real (nonordinary reality), the nagual. See nagual.

transmutation. Changing energy from one state to another, such as transforming water to ice or vapor and vice versa; changing negative, or inert, energy into positive, or active, energy; or neutralizing energy to be reabsorbed by the Earth. Ancient practices involved burying an energized object in the ground, burning it with fire, or submerging it in water.

unoli (You-Know-Lee). Cherokee, meaning literally "winds" but used as a designation for the Powers of the directions.

vibrational rate/vibrational frequency. The measurable level of energy of a person, place, or object; the higher the rate, the closer to the source, or optimal wholeness.

vision quest. A period in a desolate or isolated spot under the tutelage of a spiritual elder, intended as an opportunity for discovering the inner self, the meaning of life, or to connect with higher beings.

vortexes. Doorways or portals into other dimensions; areas where energy in flux can affect time and space.

wakan. Lakota word meaning "sacred."

Wakan-Tanka. Lakota word for Great Spirit, or the Great Mystery, God.

wand. A long, thin implement used to direct energy when pointed. Some are ornate, with carvings, feathers, beads, and similar adornments, while others are as simple as a twig or a feather.

wild spirit. A spirit of the land that usually inhabits wilderness areas away from civilization or contact with humans; ally.

will of creation. Energy of the moment, moving from one state to another; the potential to transform to another manifestation.

Bibliography

Bohm, David. *Wholeness and the Implicate Order.* Boston: Routledge & Kegan Paul, 1980.

Boyd, Doug. *Mad Bear: Spirit, Healing, and the Sacred in the Life of a Native American Medicine Man.* New York: Touchstone, 1994.

——. *Rolling Thunder.* New York: Dell, 1974.

Braden, Gregg. *Awakening to Zero Point: The Collective Initiation.* Bellevue, WA: Radio Bookstore Press, 1997.

——. *The Isaiah Effect.* New York: Harmony Books, 2000.

——. *Walking Between the Worlds: The Science of Compassion.* Bellevue, WA: Radio Bookstore Press, 1997.

Castaneda, Carlos. *The Teachings of Don Juan: A Yaqui Way of Knowledge.* New York: Ballantine, 1969.

Catches, Pete S., Sr., Peter V. Catches, ed. *Sacred Fireplace (Oceti Wakan): Life and Teachings of a Lakota Medicine Man.* Santa Fe, NM: Clear Light Publishers, 1999.

Diamant, Anita. *The Red Tent.* New York: St. Martin's Press, 1997.

Eagle Feather, Ken. *A Toltec Path.* Charlottesville, VA: Hampton Roads, 1995.

Emoto, Masaru. *The Message from Water,* vols. 1 and 2. Tokyo, Japan: Hado Kyoikusha, 2004.

Ewing, Jim PathFinder. *Clearing: A Guide to Liberating Energies Trapped in Buildings and Lands.* Findhorn, Scotland: Findhorn Press, 2006.

Harner, Michael. *The Way of the Shaman.* New York: Harper, 1980.

Ingerman, Sandra. *Medicine for the Earth: How to Transform Personal and Environmental Toxins.* New York: Three Rivers Press, 2000.

——. *Shamanic Journeying: A Beginner's Guide.* Boulder, CO: Sounds True, 2004.

——. *Soul Retrieval: Mending the Fragmented Self.* San Francisco: Harper, 1991.

——. *Welcome Home: Following Your Soul's Journey Home.* San Francisco: Harper, 1993.

Kelly, Maureen J. *Reiki and the Healing Buddha.* Twin Lakes, WI: Lotus Press, 2000.

Lungold, Ian Xel. *Mayan Calendar and Conversion Codex.* Sedona, AZ: Majix, 1999.

Mails, Thomas E. *Fools Crow.* Lincoln, NE: University of Nebraska Press, 1990.

Medicine Eagle, Brooke. *The Last Ghost Dance: A Guide for Earth Mages.* New York: Wellspring/Ballantine, 2000.

——. *Buffalo Woman Comes Singing.* New York: Ballantine Books, 1991.

Melchizedek, Drunvalo. *Ancient Secrets of the Flower of Life,* vols. 1 and 2. Flagstaff, AZ: Light Technology Publishing, 1990.

Moore, Christopher. *Coyote Blue.* New York: HarperCollins, 2004.

Neihardt, John G. *Black Elk Speaks: Being the Life Story of a Holy Man of the Oglala Sioux.* Lincoln: University of Nebraska Press, 2000.

Ruiz, Don Miguel. *The Four Agreements.* San Rafael, CA: Amber-Allen Publishing, 1997.

Sams, Jamie. *Dancing the Dream: The Seven Sacred Paths of Human Transformation.* New York: HarperCollins, 1998.

Weiss, Brian, M.D. *Messages from the Masters.* New York: Warner Books, 2000.

——. *Many Lives, Many Masters,* New York: Fireside, 1988.

Ywahoo, Dhyani. *Voices of the Ancestors: Cherokee Teachings from the Wisdom Fire.* Boston: Shambhala Publications, 1987.

About the Author

Jim PathFinder Ewing (Nvnehi Awatisgi) teaches shamanism and Reiki in Lena, Mississippi, with his wife, Annette Waya Ewing. He travels extensively, performing ceremonies and giving workshops and lectures. To contact, write:

Jim PathFinder Ewing

P.O. Box 387

Lena, MS 39094

To subscribe to his free monthly online newsletter, Keeping in Touch, visit his Web site, Healing the Earth/Ourselves, at http://www.blueskywaters.com.

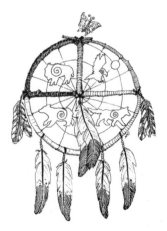